NO LONGER PRO
SEATTLE PUBLIC LIBR

WALKING ON TENERIFE

About the Author

Paddy Dillon is a prolific walker and guidebook writer, with over 60 books to his name and contributions to many more. He has also written for several outdoor magazines and appeared on radio and television.

Paddy has walked extensively around all the Canary Islands for this series of guides, along rugged cliff coasts, crossing deep and rocky *barrancos* and climbing all the highest mountains. He uses a tablet to write as he walks. This makes his descriptions, written at the very point at which the reader uses them, highly accurate and easy to follow on the ground.

Paddy is an indefatigable long-distance walker who has walked all Britain's National Trails and several major European trails. He has also walked in Nepal, Tibet and the Rocky Mountains of Canada and the US. Paddy is a member of the Outdoor Writers and Photographers Guild.

Other Cicerone guides by the author

WALKING ON TENERIFE

by

Paddy Dillon

2 POLICE SQUARE, MILNTHORPE, CUMBRIA LA7 7PY
www.cicerone.co.uk

© Paddy Dillon 2015

Second edition 2015
ISBN: 978 1 85284 793 7

First edition 2011
ISBN: 978 1 85284 599 5

Printed by KHL Printing, Singapore.
A catalogue record for this book is available from the British Library.
All photographs are by the author unless otherwise stated.

Updates to this Guide

While every effort is made by our authors to ensure the accuracy of guidebooks as they go to print, changes can occur during the lifetime of an edition. Any updates that we know of for this guide will be on the Cicerone website (www.cicerone.co.uk/793/updates), so please check before planning your trip. We also advise that you check information about such things as transport, accommodation and shops locally. Even rights of way can be altered over time. We are always grateful for information about any discrepancies between a guidebook and the facts on the ground, sent by email to info@cicerone.co.uk or by post to Cicerone, 2 Police Square, Milnthorpe LA7 7PY, United Kingdom.

Front cover: El Teide, seen from a path between El Portillo and Montaña Blanca (Walk 29)

CONTENTS

Morning mist clears above Erjos, revealing the mighty form of El Teide (Walk 13)

Map Key

════════	major roads
▬▬▬▬▬▬	walking route
••••••••••••••	walks that coincide
••• ••• ••• •••	long-distance (GR) route
▬▬ ▬▬ ▬▬	alternative route
▬ ▬ ▬ ▬	link
••••••••••••••••	dirt track
··················	seasonal river
────────	river
⬭	sea
� tunnel	tunnel
⬭	town
▲	peak
▪	habitation
●	mirador
●	fuente/spring
→	route direction
→	direction arrow
Ⓢ Ⓕ	start point/finish point
ⓢⓕ	start/finish point
Ⓐⓢ Ⓐⓕ	alternative start/alternative finish
Ⓐⓢⓕ	alternative start/finish

Contour Key

	1600–1800m		3600–3800m
	1400–1600m		3400–3600m
	1200–1400m		3200–3400m
	1000–1200m		3000–3200m
	800–1000m		2800–3000m
	600–800m		2600–2800m
	400–600m		2400–2600m
	200–400m		2200–2400m
	0–200m		2000–2200m
	sea level		1800–2000m

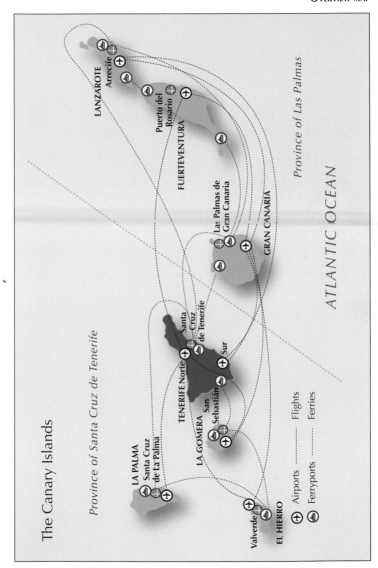

The Canary Islands

Province of Santa Cruz de Tenerife

Province of Las Palmas

ATLANTIC OCEAN

LANZAROTE
Arrecife

Puerto del Rosario

FUERTEVENTURA

Las Palmas de Gran Canaria

GRAN CANARIA

LA PALMA
Santa Cruz de La Palma

Santa Cruz de Tenerife

TENERIFE Norte

Sur

San Sebastián

LA GOMERA

Valverde

EL HIERRO

OVERVIEW MAP

Airports ———— Flights
Ferryports ········· Ferries

9

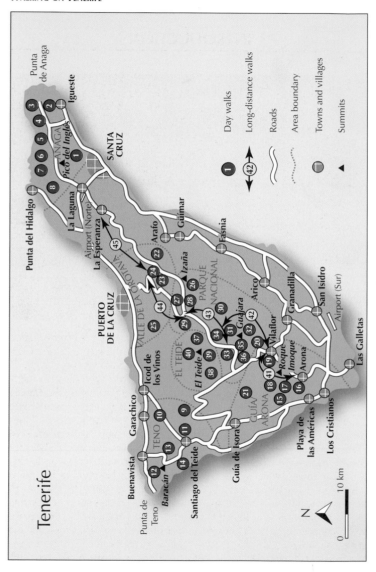

Tenerife

Day walks

Long-distance walks

Roads

Area boundary

Towns and villages

Summits

INTRODUCTION

Looking up the Barranco de Igueste, with tabaibal and cardón scrub growing thick on the slopes (Walk 2)

The seven sub-tropical Canary Islands bask in sunny splendour off the Atlantic coast of north-west Africa. Millions of sun-starved north Europeans flock there for beach holidays, but increasingly visitors are discovering the amazing variety of landscapes throughout the archipelago. Conditions range from semi-deserts to perpetually moist *laurisilva* 'cloud forests', from rugged cliff coasts to high mountains, from fertile cultivation terraces to awesome rocky *barrancos* carved deep into multi-coloured layers of volcanic bedrock. Some areas are given the highest possible protection as national parks, but there are many more types of protected landscapes, rural parks, natural monuments and nature reserves.

More and more walkers are finding their feet, exploring the Canary Islands using centuries-old mule tracks, rugged cliff paths and forest trails. Paths pick their way between cultivation terraces, squeeze between houses and make their way to rugged coves and hidden beaches. Some paths run from village to village, following old mule tracks once used to transport goods, while other paths are based on pilgrim trails to and from remote churches and *ermitas*. Many have been cleared, repaired, signposted and waymarked in recent years, ready to be explored and enjoyed.

This guidebook explores many waymarked trails on the island of Tenerife. This large island boasts routes of all types – from easy strolls to hands-on scrambling, from simple day-walks to long-distance trails. As these routes are fully signposted and waymarked, walkers can follow them with confidence and enjoy the island to the full. Almost 630km (390 miles) of trails are described in this guidebook.

LOCATION

The Canary Islands are more or less enclosed in a rectangular area from 13°30'W to 18°00'W and 27°30'N to 29°30'N. As a group, they stretch west to east over 450km (280 miles). Although administered by Spain, the mother country is 1100km (685 miles) away. The narrowest strait between the Canary Islands and Africa is a mere 110km (70 miles). The total land area is almost 7500km (2900 square miles), but the sea they occupy is 10 times that size.

GEOLOGY

Most of the world's volcanic landscapes are formed where huge continental or oceanic 'plates' collide with each other. When continental plates collide, the Earth's crust crumples upwards to form mountains, and

when plates are torn apart, basaltic rock from deep within the Earth's mantle erupts to form mountains. The Canary Islands, however, are different, and have a complicated geological history.

The African landmass is the visible part of a continental plate that extends into the Atlantic Ocean, but the Canary Islands lie within the oceanic crust of the eastern Atlantic Ocean, close to the passive junction with the African continental plate. It is thought that the islands now lie directly above a hot-spot, or mantle plume, some 2500km (1550 miles)

El Teide vents hot gases and steam from fumaroles; this one is very close to the summit (Walks 37–40)

deep within the Earth. The mantle plume is fixed, but the oceanic and African plates are drifting very slowly eastwards. Every so often a split in the oceanic crust opens above the mantle plume, allowing molten rock to vent onto the ocean floor. As more and more material erupts, it piles higher and higher until it rises from the sea. Each of the Canary Islands was formed this way.

Lanzarote and Fuerteventura were the first Canary Islands to form, and were subsequently pulled eastwards. The next time a rift opened over the mantle plume the islands of Gran Canaria and Tenerife were formed, and these were in turn pulled eastwards. A further oceanic rift led to the formation of La Gomera, La Palma and El Hierro. Looking forward in geological time more islands will appear as other rifts are torn open in the future.

The forces at work deep within the Earth can scarcely be imagined. Every single piece of rock throughout the Canary Islands once existed in a molten state. Consider the energy needed to melt one small stone, and multiply that to imagine the energy required to melt everything in the island chain, as well as the immense amount of rock beneath the sea that supports them all!

Over time huge amounts of volcanic material were piled high, but erosion has led to great instability. During recent geological time vast chunks of the islands have collapsed into the sea, creating features such as El Golfo on El Hierro, the Caldeira de Taburiente on La Palma and the Orotava valley on Tenerife. With each catastrophic collapse, tidal waves devastated places around the Atlantic Ocean. Some geologists believe that the steep, bulging northern slope of El Teide could collapse during any future volcanic eruption.

WILDLIFE

Plants and flowers

While the northern hemisphere was in the grip of an Ice Age, the Canary Islands were sluiced by rainstorms, with powerful rivers carving deep, steep-sided barrancos into unstable layers of ash and lava. As the land-masses emerged from the Ice Age the Canary Islands dried out and the vegetation had to adapt to survive. Some species are well adapted to semi-desert conditions, while on some high parts of the islands, laurisilva cloud forests are able to trap moisture from the mists and keep themselves well watered. Laurisilva forests once spread all the way round Mediterranean and tropical regions, and extensive examples of these forests thrive on Tenerife.

Canary pines flourish on high, dry mountainsides, sometimes in places where nothing else grows. A collar of pine forest, known as the Corona Forestal, surrounds the highest mountains on Tenerife. Almost every pine you see will have a scorched trunk, but they regenerate surprisingly well after forest fires. Beware of the long pine needles on the ground, as they are slippery underfoot. Canary palms also flourish in dry places, and in the past every part of the tree had a use; today they provide delicious *miel de palma*, or palm syrup. Every so often dragon trees occur, the last surviving descendants of the ancient prehistoric forests. They have been decimated in the wild but prove popular in gardens.

Tagasaste trees are often found in dense plantations, always in places where livestock are grazed. They grow with little water, yet have a high nutritional content and are regularly cut for animal fodder. In recent years they have been exported to Australia. Junipers are common; fruit and nut trees have been established, including apples, oranges, lemons, bananas, almonds, figs and vines. The introduced prickly pears are abundant, not so much for their fruit, but for raising cochineal beetles, whose blood provides a vivid red dye.

Bushy scrub is rich and varied, including sticky-leaved cistus and a host of species that walkers should learn to identify. These include bushy, rubbery *tabaibal* and the tall *cardón*, or candelabra spurge. Both have milky latex sap, as does tangled *cornical*, with its distinctive horned seed pods, which creeps over the ground and drystone walls. *Aulaga* looks like a tangled mass of spines and is often found colonising old cultivation terraces in arid areas. Aromatic,

pale green *incienso* is a bushy plant that, with *salado*, grows densely on the arid lower slopes of the islands. The fragrant Canarian lavender usually grows in arid, rocky, stony areas among other scrub species. Few of the plants have common English names, but all of them feature so often that they should be learned.

Flowers grow all year round, but visitors in spring and early summer will be amazed at the colour and wealth of flowering plants. Many are Canarian endemics, and even trying to compile a shortlist would be pointless. Anyone with a particular interest in flowers and other plants should carry a specific field guide, in English. Try *Native Flora of the Canary Islands* by Miguel Ángel Cabrera Pérez, Editorial Everest or *Wild Flowers of the Canary Islands* by David Bramwell and Zoë Bramwell, Editorial Rueda.

Animals

As befits remote islands created in relatively recent geological time, the main animal groups to colonise the land were winged creatures, insects and birds. The largest indigenous land mammals were bats. Large and small lizards also arrived, possibly clinging to driftwood. The laurisilva cloud forest is home to the laurel pigeon, while the rock pigeon prefers cliffs. Buzzards and kestrels can be spotted hunting, and ospreys are making a slow come-back. Ravens and choughs are common in some places. There are several varieties of pipits, chaffinches, warblers and chiffchaffs. One of the smallest birds is the kinglet, a relative of the goldcrest. There are canaries, which have nothing to do with the name of the islands, and parakeets that add a flash of colour. The islands attract plenty of passage migrants, as well as escapees from aviaries. The coastal fringes are colonised by gulls, but it is best to take a boat trip to spot shearwaters or storm petrels, as they spend most of their time on open water. Boat trips are also the way to spot a variety of dolphins and whales.

Once the Guanche people arrived and colonised the islands over two thousand years ago, the forests suffered as much from clearance as from grazing by voracious sheep and goats. Following the Conquest in the 15th century, the Spaniards brought other domestic animals; of these the cats had a particularly devastating impact on the native wildlife, practically wiping out giant Canarian lizards, which have only recently been rescued from the edge of extinction. The largest lizards on Tenerife are slightly speckled with blue. Rabbits chew their way through the vegetation and appear regularly on Canarian menus.

NATIONAL PARKS

The Canary Islands contain a handful of national parks and many other protected areas. The Parque Nacional del Teide is in the middle of Tenerife, embracing the highest peaks. Other protected areas on the island include Parque Rural (Rural

Lizards can be observed on many parts of Tenerife whenever the sun shines strongly

Park), Parque Natural (Natural Park), Paisaje Protegido (Protected Land), Reserva Natural Especial (Special Nature Reserve), Monumento Natural (Natural Monument), and so on. Prominent notices usually tell walkers when they are entering or leaving these areas. Very little territory lies outside one of these places! There are visitor centres where more information can be studied, and where interesting literature is on sale.

THE FORTUNATE ISLES

Myths and legends speak of 'The Fortunate Isles', or 'Isles of the Blessed', lying somewhere in the Atlantic, enjoying a wonderful climate and bearing all manner of fruit. The rebel Roman general Sertorius planned to retire there, while Plutarch referred to them many times, though Pliny warned 'these islands, however, are greatly annoyed by the putrefying bodies of monsters, which are constantly thrown up by the sea'. Maybe these scribes knew of the Canary Islands, or maybe they were drawing on older Phoenician or Carthaginian references. Some would even claim that the islands were the last remnants of Atlantis.

The Gaunches, often described as a 'stone-age' civilisation, settled on the Canary Islands well over 2000 years ago, and Cro-Magnon Man was there as early as 3000BC. No-one knows where the Guanches came from, but it seems likely that they arrived from North Africa in fleets of canoes.

Although technologically primitive, their society was well-ordered, and they had a special regard for monumental rock-forms in the mountains.

The Guanches fiercely resisted the well-armed Spaniards during the 15th century Conquest of the islands, but one by one each island fell. Tenerife capitulated last of all, with the mighty volcano of El Teide grumbling throughout. Many Guanches were slaughtered or enslaved, but some entered into treaties, converted to Christianity and inter-married. They lost their land and freedom, but their blood flows in the veins of native Canarios.

The Canary Islands were visited by Christopher Columbus on his voyage of discovery in 1492. Subsequently they were used as stepping stones to the Americas, and many Canarios emigrated. The islands were exposed and not always defended with military might; they were subject to pirate raids, endured disputes with the Portuguese, were attacked by the British and suffered wavering economic fortunes.

There was constant rivalry between Tenerife and Gran Canaria, with the entire island group being governed from Las Palmas de Gran Canaria from 1808, before Santa Cruz de Tenerife became the capital in 1822. In 1927 the Canary Islands were divided into two provinces – Las Palmas and Santa Cruz de Tenerife.

In the early 20th century the military governor of the Canary Islands, General Franco, launched a military coup from Tenerife. His subsequent victory in the infamous Civil War was followed by a long repressive dictatorship. The Canary Islands remained free of the worst strife of the war, but also became something of a backwater. It was largely as a result of Franco's later policies that the Canary Islands were developed in the 1960s as a major destination for northern Europeans.

Since 1982 the islands have been an autonomous region and there have been calls for complete independence from Spain. The islanders regard themselves as 'Canarios' first and 'Spanish' second, though they are also fiercely loyal to their own particular islands, towns and villages.

GETTING THERE

There are plenty of direct flights to Tenerife, scheduled or charter, from a range of British and European airports. The hardest part is checking all the 'deals' to find an airport, operator, schedules and prices that suit. Most international flights land at Tenerife Sur, though a few land at Tenerife Norte.

Frequent, fast and cheap TITSA buses link Tenerife Sur with the bustling nearby resorts of Los Cristianos and Playa de las Américas, and some services also run to the capital city of Santa Cruz. From Tenerife Norte, regular buses run to Santa Cruz and the northern resort of Puerto de la Cruz.

The most spectacular walking area on Tenerife, in the national park, has only one expensive hotel

The best time to visit Tenerife and enjoy its wealth of flowers is early in spring

have no problem turning up unannounced on the doorsteps of hotels and pensións and securing accommodation. It is also possible to take short self-catering lets with ease. Simply obtain an up-to-date accommodation list from a tourist information office as soon as you reach the island. Opportunities to camp are very limited; camping is not allowed in the national park, where there is only an expensive hotel. Wild camping is technically illegal, but it does take place.

WHEN TO GO

Most people visit the Canary Islands in summer, but it is usually too hot for walking. Winter weather is often good, but on Tenerife expect some cloud cover and rain on the mid-slopes, as well as snow on the highest parts. Spring weather is sunny and clear; the vegetation is fresh and features an amazing wealth of flowers. Autumn weather is often good, but the vegetation often seems rather scorched after the summer.

ACCOMMODATION

Most visitors to the Canary Islands opt for a package deal, so they are tied to a single accommodation base in a faceless resort. This is far from ideal and a base in the 'wrong' place can make it difficult to get to and from walking routes. Out of season, walkers would

HEALTH AND SAFETY

There are no nasty diseases on the Canary Islands, or, at least, nothing you couldn't contract at home. Water on Tenerife is either drawn from rainfall, or generated by the laurisilva cloud forests. It soaks into the ground, is filtered through thick beds of volcanic ash and emerges pure and clean, perfectly safe to drink. Desalinated seawater is also produced, which is perfectly safe to drink, though some people dislike the taste. Bottled water is available if you prefer, but buy it cheaply from supermarkets rather than at considerable expense from bars. There are no snakes, no stinging insects worse than honey-bees, and there are always warning signs near hives. Don't annoy dogs and they won't annoy you. Dogs that are likely to bite are nearly always tethered, so keep away.

Remember that the highest mountain on Tenerife, El Teide, rises to 3718m (12,198ft). This is higher than anything in mainland Spain, and high enough to cause altitude sickness. Visitors are warned of this when they use the *teleférico* for the ascent, and some people do react badly. The 'cure' is to descend immediately, which can be a problem when the *teleférico* is busy. Walkers who take the time to complete walks at ever-higher altitudes should have no problem building themselves up for a strenuous climb up El Teide.

In case of a medical emergency, dial 112 for an ambulance. In case of a non-emergency, Tenerife has hospitals, health centres (*Centro de Salud*) and chemists (*Farmacia*). If treatment is required, EU citizens should present their European Health Insurance Card, which may help to offset some costs.

FOOD AND DRINK

Every town and most of the villages throughout the Canary Islands have bars. Most bars also double as cafés or restaurants, often serving tapas, which are often in glass cabinets, so you can point to the ones you want to eat. There are also shops, selling local and imported foodstuffs. Always make the effort to sample local fare, which is often interesting and very tasty. The availability of refreshments is mentioned on every walking trail, but bear in mind that opening hours are variable. Some shops take a very long lunch break, and not all businesses are open

Water abstraction and supply is a complicated process on Tenerife

every day of the week. Some shops are closed all weekend, or at least half of Saturday and all of Sunday.

LANGUAGE

Castilian Spanish is spoken throughout the Canary Islands, though in most resorts and large hotels there are English and German speakers. Those who travel to remote rural parts will need at least a few basic phrases of Spanish. Anyone with any proficiency in Spanish will quickly realise that the Canarios have their own accent and colloquialisms. For instance, the letter 's' often vanishes from the middle or end of words, to be replaced by a gentle 'h', or even a completely soundless gap. '*Los Cristianos*', for example, becomes '*Loh Cri-tiano*'. A bus is referred to as an *autobus* in Spain, but as a *guagua* throughout the Canary Islands. Some natives may seize the opportunity to practise their English with you, while others may be puzzled by your command of Spanish. No matter how bad you think you sound, you will not be the worst they've heard!

MONEY

The Euro is the currency of the Canary Islands. Large denomination Euro notes are difficult to use for small purchases, so avoid the €500 and €200 notes altogether, and avoid the €100 notes if you can. The rest are fine: €50, €20, €10 and €5. Coins come in €2 and €1. Small denomination coins come in values of 50c, 20c, 10c, 5c, 2c and 1c. Banks and ATMs are mentioned where they occur, if cash is needed. Many accommodation providers accept major credit and debit cards, as will large supermarkets, but small bars, shops and cafés deal only in cash.

COMMUNICATIONS

All the towns and some of the villages have post offices (*Correos*) and public telephones. Opening times for large post offices are usually 0830–1430 Monday to Friday, 0930–1300 Saturday, closed on Sunday. Small post offices have more limited opening times. Mobile phone coverage is usually good in towns and villages, but can be completely absent elsewhere, depending on the nature of the terrain. High mountains and deep barrancos block signals. Wi-fi internet access is usually offered by hotels but, if relying on it, please check when making a booking.

WALKING ON TENERIFE

*El Teide stands high above the clouds, experiencing different
weather from the rest of the island*

This is the largest of the Canary Islands, in the middle of the archipelago. The southern part of the island is arid and often environmentally degraded, having been intensively cultivated and then abandoned as water supplies ran out. Walking opportunities are limited, and most visitors travel through the southern parts at speed on busy roads, not inclined to stop. The northern part of the island, by contrast, is moist, fresh and green, often terraced and intensively cultivated, with good walking routes available. The extreme ends of Tenerife, Anaga in the northeast and Teno in the north-west, are the oldest parts of the island, riven by deep barrancos, with cliffs and arid slopes rising to summits covered in laurisilva forest.

The most popular resorts, along with the bulk of accommodation on Tenerife, are based around Los Cristianos and Playa de las Américas in the south, and Puerto de la Cruz in the north. There are good walking opportunities within easy travelling distance of these resorts. Anaga has an impressive network of signposted and waymarked trails, and Teno is almost as good in that respect.

The central part of Tenerife is completely dominated by a huge, rugged and steep-sided volcanic peak – El Teide. This is in turn surrounded by a semi-circle of jagged peaks, the remains of a vast volcanic caldera. The whole central area of Tenerife is protected as a national park and boasts a wealth of interesting and sometimes very rugged trails. The altitude is generally well above 2000m (6560ft), and the region often basks in the sun under a blue sky when other parts of the island are covered in cloud, or experiencing rain. However, when bad weather hits these mountains, it is often very bad, and extensive snow cover can make it difficult to follow some routes in winter.

It takes time to explore Tenerife, and some people return year after year to discover more and more of the island. This guidebook contains a good six weeks of walking, and to make the most of opportunities visitors should be prepared to choose different bases to explore different areas; otherwise too much time could be spent travelling to far-flung parts. Good fast roads encircle the island and climb remarkably high, but other roads are narrow and convoluted and can only be travelled slowly.

The 45 days of walking on Tenerife described in this guidebook are made up of 40 one-day walks, either signposted as PR (*pequeño recorrido*) routes or number-coded *senderos* in the national park, plus another five days signposted as a GR (*gran recorrido*) route that can be linked together as a long-distance walk. Few of these routes stand in isolation, and most of them link with one, two or more adjacent routes, so there are options to modify and adapt them, and some routes feature variants and extensions. There are almost 630km (390 miles) of trails described on Tenerife in this book, and this represents only part of the signposted and waymarked trail network.

GETTING THERE

By Air

Most visitors fly direct to Tenerife Sur airport, from the UK or Europe, using a variety of airlines. Local flights from the adjacent Canary Islands land at Tenerife Norte, and are operated by Binter Canarias, tel. 902-391392, www.bintercanarias.com, or Canaryfly, tel. 902-808065, www.canaryfly.es.

Frequent, fast and cheap TITSA buses link Tenerife Sur with the bustling nearby resorts of Los Cristianos and Playa de las Américas, and some services also run to the capital city of Santa Cruz. From Tenerife Norte, regular buses run to Santa Cruz and the northern resort of Puerto de la Cruz. Taxis are also available at the airports.

By Ferry

Two ferry companies operate between Tenerife and neighbouring islands. Lineas Fred Olsen, tel. 902-100107, www.fredolsen.es, is quick and expensive. Naviera Armas, tel. 902-456500, www.naviera-armas.com, is slower and cheaper. Ferries berth at Los Cristianos, from the westernmost islands of La Gomera, La Palma and El Hierro, and at Santa Cruz, from Gran Canaria.

GETTING AROUND

By Bus

Tenerife has an excellent network of bus services operated by Transportes

TITSA buses operate all over Tenerife from sea level to almost 2400m (7875ft) at the foot of El Teide

Interurbanos de Tenerife SA (TITSA), tel. 922-531300, www.titsa.com. Obtain an up-to-date timetable for the whole island as soon as possible, from bus stations or information kiosks. There are two timetables, one listing all services and another listing only those regularly used by tourists. Details can also be checked on the website. Tickets are for single or day return journeys and fares are paid on boarding the bus. For the best deal, obtain a pre-paid *bono* ticket and use the on-board machine. The *bono* will be debited less than what you would pay for a ticket on board. Buses are referred to as *guaguas*, although bus stops, or *paradas*, may be marked as 'bus'.

By Taxi

Long taxi rides are expensive, but short journeys are worth considering. Taxi ranks are located in all the towns and some of the villages. Fares are fixed by the municipalities and can be inspected on demand, though negotiation might be possible.

Car Hire

Some people will automatically pick up a hire car in Tenerife, and this is easily arranged in advance or on arrival. In some instances, a car is useful to reach a walk in a remote location, and using a car might sometimes offer more flexibility than using bus services. However, some of the best walks on Tenerife are linear, and if you park a car at one end it can be very difficult to return to it.

Planning your Transport

To make the most of walking opportunities, and limit long and awkward travelling, it is best to choose a number of accommodation bases with good bus connections. Linear routes described in this book generally start at the higher end and finish at the lower end, but there are exceptions. Where buses serve both ends, timetable details need to be checked, and you need to pace yourself to fit in with the schedules. In the few places where bus services are extremely limited, or completely absent, the only options are to arrange drop-offs and pick-ups, either by taxi or by arrangement with a car-driving friend. Pick-ups require careful planning and timing so as not to inconvenience or alarm those who are waiting for you.

WHAT TO TAKE

If planning to use one or two bases to explore, then a simple day pack is all you need, containing items you would normally take for a day walk. Waterproofs can be lightweight and might not even be used. Footwear is a personal preference, but wear what you would normally wear for steep, rocky, stony slopes, remembering that hot feet are more likely to be a problem than wet feet. Lightweight light-coloured clothing is best in bright sunshine, along with a sun hat and frequent applications of sunscreen.

If snow and ice covers the highest mountains, warmer and more protective clothing will be needed, possibly even ice axe and crampons. If planning to backpack around the island, bear in mind that wild camping is technically illegal, though surprisingly popular. Lightweight kit should be carried, as a heavy pack is a cruel burden on steep slopes in hot weather. Water can be difficult to find, so try to anticipate your needs and carry enough to last until you reach a village, bar or houses where you can obtain a refill.

WAYMARKING AND ACCESS

Tenerife only recently adopted a system for signposting and waymarking routes using standard European codes. The island has a network of short PR (*pequeño recorrido*) routes, which are marked with yellow and white paint flashes, and numbered to keep them separate. Signposts will read 'PR TF…', with a number following the letters. These codes are quoted in the route descriptions so that walkers will always

Red and white flashes mark the GR 131, and yellow and white flashes mark the shorter PR routes

be able to check that they are going the right way. There are also GR (*gran recorrido*) routes, which are intended as long-distance walks, but can also serve as simple one-day linear walks. Some short links are marked as SL (*sendero local*), literally 'local walk'.

Apart from signposts, routes are marked by occasional paint marks, parallel yellow and white stripes for the PR routes, with red and white stripes for the GR routes and green and white stripes for the SL routes. These confirm that walkers are still on course, and usually appear at junctions. Left and right turns are indicated with right-angled flashes, but if the paint marks form an 'X', this indicates that a wrong turn has been made.

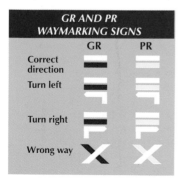

GR AND PR WAYMARKING SIGNS		
	GR	**PR**
Correct direction		
Turn left		
Turn right		
Wrong way		

The national park, Parque Nacional del Teide, has for many years used its own method to mark a splendid network of routes, generally using metal plaques fixed to rocks. These plaques bear the word *sendero* followed by a number that can be checked against map-boards and route maps produced by the national park authority.

MAPS

The Instituto Geográfico Nacional (IGN), www.cnig.es, publishes maps of the Canary Islands at scales of 1:50,000 and 1:25,000. These are part of the Mapa Topográfico Nacional (MTN) series. To avoid disappointment, please check the style and quality of these maps before making a purchase, since they generally do not show the sort of details that walkers require.

On Tenerife, good maps suitable for exploring are rather limited. There is the excellent 1:25,000 'Teide Parque Nacional' map, stretching well beyond the national park in the middle of the island. For complete coverage of Tenerife on one sheet, the next best map is the 1:50,000 Kompass map of Tenerife, and this is available in Britain with an Automobile Association cover, as the AA Island Series 11 – Tenerife. The evolving trail network does not yet feature on maps, though routes are usually outlined on map-boards around the island, from which details can be copied and transferred to other maps.

Maps can be ordered in advance from British suppliers such as Stanfords (12–14 Long Acre, London,

Mapboards, signposts and waymarks have appeared where old paths have been restored

WC2E 9BR, tel. 0207 836 1321, www.stanfords.co.uk), The Map Shop (15 High Street, Upton-upon-Severn, WR8 0HJ, tel. 01684 593146, www.themapshop.co.uk) or Cordee (www.cordee.co.uk).

The sketch maps in this guide-book are at a scale of 1:50,000. Routes marked on them can be transferred to other maps if required.

FOOD AND DRINK

Tenerife is self-sufficient in terms of fruit, vegetables and fish. While some restaurants are cosmopolitan, others offer good local fare. Specialities include goat cheese. Wrinkly potatoes (*papas arrugadas*) cooked in salt are surprisingly refreshing in hot weather, served with hot *mojo roja* sauce and gentler *mojo verde*. The most popular fish dishes are based on *vieja*. If any dishes such as soups or stews need thickening, reach for the roasted flour *gofio*, which also serves as a breakfast cereal. Local wines are also available. Never pass an opportunity to indulge in local fare!

TOURIST INFORMATION OFFICES

- Tenerife Sur Airport, tel. 922-392037
- Tenerife Norte Airport, tel. 922-635192
- Intercambiador (Bus Station) Santa Cruz, tel. 922-533353

- Santa Cruz (Cabildo), tel. 922-239592
- La Laguna, tel. 922-632718
- Candelaria, tel. 922-032230
- Garachico, tel. 922-133461
- Los Cristianos, tel. 922-757137
- Buenavista del Norte, tel. 922-127192
- Icod de los Vinos, tel. 922-812123
- La Orotava, tel. 922-323041
- Puerto de la Cruz, tel. 922-388777
- Puerto de la Cruz, tel. 922-386000

EMERGENCIES

The pan-European emergency telephone number 112 is used to call for assistance throughout the Canary Islands, linking with the police, fire or ambulance service, for a response on land or at sea. The Guardia Civil telephone number is 062, and it is likely they would be involved in a response involving mountain rescue, as they generally patrol rural areas.

USING THIS GUIDE

The walks are spread around the island, and where they lie side-by-side, links between routes are possible. Routes are described on the Anaga peninsula in the north-east, followed by those on the Teno peninsula in the north-west. Routes are then described between Guía, Arona and Vilaflor, handy for the resorts of Playa

Workmen restoring an old zigzag path on part of the long-distance GR 131 (Walk 45)

de las Américas and Los Cristianos in the south. To the north, routes in the Valle de la Orotava are handy for Puerto de la Cruz. The highest and wildest routes are in the Parque Nacional de Teide, where routes onto El Teide are described separately. Finally, the GR 131 trail is described as a five-day long-distance walk from Arona to La Esperanza. This route can of course be followed as a series of linear day-walks broken at intervals.

On arrival on Tenerife, visit a tourist information office as soon as possible and ask for an accommodation list, and any information about walking opportunities that they stock. Remember to pick up leaflets about any visitor attractions that seem interesting, as they usually give full contact details, opening times and admission charges. Visit a bus station or bus information kiosk for an up-to-date bus timetable. After that, you should have all the information you need to enjoy the walks to the maximum!

ANAGA

Anaga, one of the oldest parts of Tenerife, is riven by deep and steep-sided barrancos

The Anaga peninsula, in the extreme north-east, is one of the oldest parts of Tenerife, and is protected as the Parque Rural de Anaga. Its rugged coastline often features cliffs, its mountains are riven by deep, steep-sided barrancos and the highest parts are covered in dense laurisilva cloud forests. Small villages cling to steep slopes that have been terraced for cultivation, and a network of old paths and mule tracks, as well as convoluted roads, link one village with another. Many routes have been signposted and waymarked in recent years.

Eight walks are offered on the peninsula and, while each one stands on its own merit as a day walk, they could also be linked together to create a long-distance walk around the peninsula. While the nearby urban areas of Santa Cruz and La Laguna offer plenty of accommodation, walkers also have the option of staying at a hostel high in the mountains at El Bailadero; the Albergue Montes de Anaga, tel. 922-823225, www.alberguestenerife.net.

There is an interesting visitor centre at Cruz del Carmen, dedicated to the natural history of the Anaga peninsula, tel. 922-633576. It offers plenty of information about walking opportunities in the area. Buses serve the villages on the peninsula from Santa Cruz and La Laguna.

WALK 1
Pico del Inglés to Valleseco

Start	Pico del Inglés
Finish	La Quebrada or Valleseco, near Santa Cruz
Distance	7 or 9km (4½ or 5½ miles)
Total Ascent	30m (100ft)
Total Descent	960m (3150ft)
Time	3hrs
Terrain	Mostly good paths and mostly downhill, but occasionally rugged. The final stretch is on a road.
Refreshment	Bars at Valleseco.
Transport	Occasional buses from La Laguna to Pico del Inglés. Regular buses from Valleseco to Santa Cruz.
Waymarked route(s)	Route uses PR TF 2.

The 'English Peak' can be reached by bus. A relatively straightforward route runs down to Valleseco in the suburbs of Santa Cruz. The lush laurisilva forest on the mountains gives way to scrub more suited to arid conditions further downhill, as the route drops into a deep barranco.

There are occasional buses to **Pico del Inglés**, around 1000m (3280ft) high, and if these are not convenient, other buses pass 1km (½ mile) from a car park and *mirador* near the summit. Despite nearby masts there are splendid views of the Anaga peninsula, the urban sprawl of Santa Cruz and La Laguna, with El Teide rising beyond. Gran Canaria lies out to sea. The peak was named after a visitor who fell to his death; only he wasn't an Englishman, but an Austrian.

From the **Pico del Inglés** car park a signpost for Valleseco points down a short flight of steps. Turn left and right past a derelict building; then the path is often worn to bedrock on a slope of laurisilva woodland. Keep ahead at a junction, along the clearest path, flashed yellow/white. Occasional views to either side reveal that the route is along a rocky crest, rising and falling. There is a

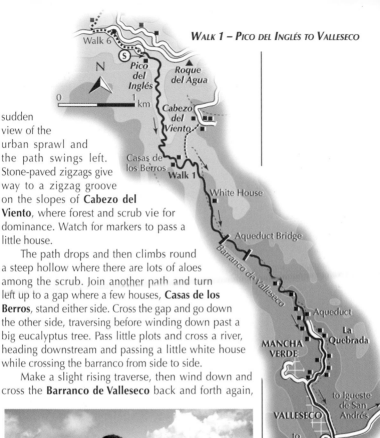

sudden view of the urban sprawl and the path swings left. Stone-paved zigzags give way to a zigzag groove on the slopes of **Cabezo del Viento**, where forest and scrub vie for dominance. Watch for markers to pass a little house.

The path drops and then climbs round a steep hollow where there are lots of aloes among the scrub. Join another path and turn left up to a gap where a few houses, **Casas de los Berros**, stand either side. Cross the gap and go down the other side, traversing before winding down past a big eucalyptus tree. Pass little plots and cross a river, heading downstream and passing a little white house while crossing the barranco from side to side.

Make a slight rising traverse, then wind down and cross the **Barranco de Valleseco** back and forth again,

The Roque de Agua is seen on the way down from Pico del Inglés

In wet weather waterfalls can be seen at intervals through the Barranco de Valleseco

passing a concrete **aqueduct**. Cross the barranco later and pass a **bridge** carrying another aqueduct, spanning an impressive narrow rock gorge. Cross again well below the bridge, then back again. Pass stoutly-walled plots and cross yet again. Pass more plots and keep left below a house. Cross the river a couple more times, pass a ramshackle house, then see lots more houses straggling down through the barranco ahead. Follow the rugged path and join a concrete road beneath a concrete **aqueduct**. The road offers rapid onward progress, but the path slices up to the right and comes down later, beside a map-board and signpost.

Continue down the road, crossing two bridges and passing bus stops at **La Quebrada**. Unless a bus is due, keep walking down the road through Valleseco, passing sports facilities and bars. Reach a junction with a very busy coastal road where there are plenty of buses to and from Santa Cruz.

WALK 2
Igueste de San Andrés to Chamorga

Start	Igueste de San Andrés
Finish	Chamorga
Distance	10km (6¼ miles)
Total Ascent	875m (2870ft)
Total Descent	425m (1395ft)
Time	5hrs
Terrain	A road walk is followed by a rugged path climbing to a ridge. Intricate paths lead from village to village.
Refreshment	Bars at Igueste and Chamorga.
Transport	Regular daily buses serve Igueste de San Andrés from Santa Cruz. Infrequent buses serve Lomo de las Bodegas and Chamorga from Santa Cruz.
Waymarked route(s)	Route uses PR TF 5.

This route could be used as the first stage on a trek round the Anaga peninsula, though it stands on its own merit as a fine day's walk. After climbing through a barranco, a ridge leads to laurisilva forest, followed by a walk from the village of Lomo de las Bodegas to Chamorga.

The road serving **Igueste de San Andrés** bends round a barranco and this walk starts at its furthest point inland, where there is a bus shelter beside an ATM. Follow the road signposted 'Pista Hoya de los Juncos', which climbs from the village, crossing and re-crossing the **Barranco de Igueste**. Pass a few houses and enter the Parque Rural Anaga. The barranco bed supports dense canes and aloes, while the steep and rugged slopes rising from it are thick with tabaibal and cardón.

Turn right as marked up a steep concrete track with a 10kph speed limit. Turn left off it along a level path past little terraces, passing an old sign reading 'Casillas'. The path climbs a steep rugged slope, and a couple of little houses can be seen tucked into hollows. The scrub features tabaibal, cardón, prickly pears and asphodel, as well as fragrant incienso and lavender. The path levels out on a ridge, **Lomo de la Zapata**, with a view back to Igueste and the sea, as well as up to the well-wooded crest of the mountains.

Las Casillas, where partly-ruined houses huddle together in a gap on a rugged mountain crest

Start climbing up the ridge, but drift left and watch for yellow/white markers while climbing higher. Pass a huddle of heather trees and zig-zag up past a stump of rock. The path eventually reaches a rocky crest bearing a line of telegraph poles. Turn left and use these as giant waymarks, revealing a rugged path making a rising traverse past rampant bushy scrub. Cross a rocky gap and follow the path through a bit of laurisilva woodland. Climb a little and later go down past **Las Casillas**, where a huddle of buildings, partly ruined, lie just off the ridge around 635m (2085ft).

Follow the path close to the ridge and pass just to the right of a pylon on a gap. The path climbs, then mostly runs down across a slope of laurisilva, passing a couple of houses. Rise and fall, in and out of laurisilva, and climb through dense woods to a road junction (bus service). The road left seems to wind forever up to El Bailadero. The road downhill is for Chamorga. The road immediately to the right runs to a little **cemetery**, around 635m (2085ft).

Pass the cemetery and walk along a short track. Keep right to follow a path that leads quickly through woods and across a scrub-covered slope, passing a couple of small cultivated plots. The path reaches a slight gap on a rocky ridge. Turn left downhill,

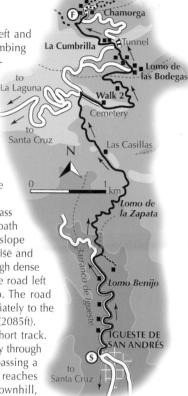

Looking across to Lomo de las Bodegas and the skyline hamlet of La Cumbrilla

35

watching carefully for a path that drifts left and passes below a building to reach the end of a track. Follow the track downhill, across a valley and up to a road in the village of **Lomo de las Bodegas**.

Turn right to reach the road-end and turn left down steps towards a chapel. However, turn left again along a concrete path, gently up and down. Don't go down a concrete path on the right, but keep straight ahead, winding uphill, with lots and lots of steps. These are flashed yellow/white all the way and occasionally named 'Camino La Cumbrilla'. The path runs along a mountain ridge with houses strung along it at **La Cumbrilla**, around 700m (2300ft). Watch for markers all the way and turn right between the last buildings.

Follow a path down through laurisilva. Keep left at a fork, past a cultivated plot, then back into the woods, rising and falling gently. A steep and greasy stone-paved zigzag path drops down an open slope and heads back into the woods. Turn right at a signposted junction to drop from the woods to land on a road near the bus stop and little chapel in **Chamorga**, around 500m (1640ft). There are lots of dragon trees around the village, and a bar. ◄

Walk 3 starts here.

WALK 3
Chamorga, El Draguillo and Almáciga

Start	Chamorga
Finish	Almáciga
Distance	16km (10 miles)
Total Ascent	300m (985ft)
Total Descent	800m (2625ft)
Time	5hrs
Terrain	Paths are often rugged and sometimes traverse steep, rocky slopes.
Refreshment	Bars at Chamorga, Benijo and Almáciga.
Transport	Infrequent buses serve Chamorga from Santa Cruz. Regular daily buses serve Almáciga from Santa Cruz.
Waymarked route(s)	Route uses PR TF 6, 6.1 and 6.2.

This route wanders round the extreme north-eastern end of Tenerife. There are two options to start, either by heading down a rugged barranco and climbing to a lighthouse, or crossing a mountain and descending to the lighthouse. The continuation is along a rugged coastal route.

Note the number of dragon trees around **Chamorga**, and start from the bar, Casa Alvaro. There are two options for reaching the lighthouse, Faro de Anaga, either by walking down the barranco via the PR TF 6, or climbing above the bar and crossing the mountainside via the PR TF 6.1.

A footbridge across the stream in the Barranco de Roque Bermejo

PR TF 6

The road has a metal fence to the right, which continues down a concrete path with steps, passing houses. Cross a footbridge, go down a path with more steps and cross another footbridge. A narrow path follows a streambed, joining a broader path which is actually the continuation of the road. Turn right to follow it and later note a little house on the left. The path becomes more rugged as it descends through the **Barranco de Roque Bermejo**, either stone-paved or on bare rock. There is a big cave up to the left as the path climbs over a rocky notch.

Go down stone steps and a stone-paved path, over a rocky hump, then down to cross a couple of wooded footbridges over a

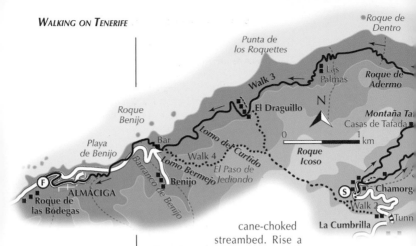

Roque Bermejo is
framed in the mouth
of the barranco.

cane-choked
streambed. Rise a
little and go round a corner, then down a
winding path. ◄ The **Casas Blancas** are in ruins, so keep
walking downhill, squeezing between cultivated areas, to
reach a signpost at the bottom. The route turns left, but
it is worth turning right first, down to houses at **Roque
Bermejo**, climbing back afterwards. Turning left leads up
a sweeping zigzag track, gravelly, gritty or stone-paved,
up crumbling slopes covered in tabaibal, to the lighthouse of **Faro de Anaga**, at 230m (755ft). Continue up to
a junction with the PR TF 6.1 and keep right.

PR TF 6.1

This route from **Chamorga** saves 2km (1½ miles), but does
not visit Roque Bermejo. Leave the bar and go up a concrete road, which quickly ends and gives way to a rugged
path. This climbs across a scrub-covered slope and keeps
left of a curious outcrop of rock. An easy stretch undulates
through laurisilva woods, rises with steps, and zigzags up
a rock face with a fence beside at a higher level. Walk to a
gap where the ruined **Casas de Tafada** stand, with patchy
laurisilva around. The path rises a little on the mountain
crest then heads left into the laurisilva. Trees give way to
a scrub-covered slope as the path winds down to a junction near the **Faro de Anaga**. Turn left to continue along
the PR TF 6.

Punta Bajo
Las Palmas

Faro de Anaga

Casas
Blancas

Roque Bermejo

Punta
El Jurado

de Roque Bermejo

The path undulates and winds easily across the slope, past fennel and tangled scrub. Pass beneath an overhang and later go round into a gully where there is a little shrine. Cross a crumbling slope and pass overhangs. Climb a

Roque Bermejo seen from the lower part of the Barranco de Roque Bermejo

39

Roque de Dentro is a sacred Guanche burial site.

little, then wind down past a building with a wine press, and down past a cave beneath a huge boulder. Go in and out of a couple of gullies, getting close-up views of the islets of **Roque de Dentro**. ◄ Climb through a barranco full of aloes to reach **Las Palmas de Anaga**, and pass the buildings with care as the cliffs beneath are crumbling.

There are lots of aloes, while prickly pears are almost like trees. Cross a couple of barrancos close together. The path winds and climbs steeply and ruggedly to outflank a crumbling cliff, heading in and out of gullies, then generally on a downward traverse. Cross a scree slope and turn up around a corner for a view of villages ahead. The path heads down across a slope and easily crosses a steep boulder scree slope. Wind downhill, with some stone steps, to cross a streambed. A short climb reaches a signpost at a junction with a track at a dragon tree beside the hamlet of **El Draguillo**, at 170m (560ft). ◄

A left turn links with Walk 4 and can be extended to return to Chamorga.

Follow the track between the houses, then go down a concrete road to leave the hamlet. Turn a corner, and apart from a stretch of dirt road over a crest, it is mostly downhill to a junction with a tarmac road at **Benijo** (bar on the right, Restaurante El Mirador). Turn right and squeeze past it to find a path down to a bouldery beach. Turn left to pick a way along the beach and cross the mouth of the **Barranco de Benijo**. Follow the marked path onwards, which rejoins the road and passes the black ash **Playa de Benijo**, popular with surfers. Use another path to avoid a further stretch of road.

When the road is joined again, turn right to follow it only for a few paces, then turn left along a concrete path with a street lamp and masses of tamarisk alongside. Zigzag up a scrub-covered slope and go up concrete steps into **Almáciga**. Climb along tarmac roads, including the gentle Calle La Renta and the steep Calle La Cruz. ◄ Reach a bus stop before a signposted fork in Calle Las Piedrillas. Turn right down a tarmac road to the beach, where there are a few bar restaurants and a bus stop at **Roque de las Bodegas**.

A shop and bar are not obvious in the village.

WALK 4
Almáciga, Benijo and El Draguillo

Start/Finish	Almáciga
Distance	10km (6¼ miles)
Total Ascent/Descent	500m (1640ft)
Time	3hrs
Terrain	Easy coastal road and hillside paths that can be steep and rugged.
Refreshment	Bars at Almáciga and Benijo.
Transport	Regular daily buses serve Almáciga from Santa Cruz.
Waymarked route(s)	Route uses PR TF 6,

This short circular walk links the coastal villages of Almáciga, Benijo and El Draguillo, then climbs to a junction where scrub-covered slopes meet the fringe of laurisilva forest. There is an option to cross a gap to reach Chamorga; otherwise the walk descends to return to Benijo and Almáciga.

Buses run to and from **Almáciga** but terminate there, so the coastal road must be followed eastwards on foot. There is no need to follow its bendy course beyond the black ash beach of **Playa de Benijo**. Use a combination of coastal path and beach walk to cross the mouth of the **Barranco de Benijo**. Watch for a path on the right to climb to the **Restaurante El Mirador** and rejoin the road. Turn left to leave the tarmac road and follow the Pista al Draguillo, PR TF 6.2, away from **Benijo**. The road is mostly concrete, and apart from a stretch of dirt road over a rise, it is mostly uphill to the hamlet of **El Draguillo**, at 170m (560ft). Follow a

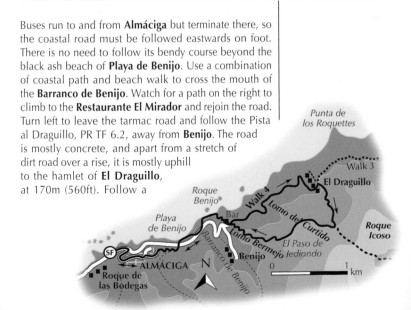

Keep left and keep climbing to follow the PR TF 6 over a well-wooded gap to Chamorga.

track to a junction where there is a signpost near a dragon tree.

Turn right and follow a path signposted as the PR TF 6 up past old terraces, becoming more rugged on a steep, scrub-covered slope. Keep climbing to reach a signposted path junction at the lower edge of laurisilva woods. ◄ Turn right as signposted for the PR TF 6.3 to Benijo.

The path runs gently downhill then rises over a rocky notch beside a rock outcrop. Head generally downhill along an airy path that may be stony, stone-paved, rock or earth as it zigzags. There is a view of villages ahead, and a wealth of wonderfully fragrant scrub. A short, steep, stone-paved climb leads through a makeshift gate at El Paso de Jediondo, then the descent continues. The path winds down below rocky outcrops, then follows an arid crest dominated by tabaibal. The path later drops onto **Lomo Bermejo** and a right turn leads down to a road junction beside the bar, Restaurante El Mirador, at **Benijo**. At this point, retrace the earlier steps of the day back to **Almáciga**.

An awesome cliff coast, seen after stormy weather, near Almáciga

WALK 5

Taganana, Afur and La Cumbre

Start/Finish	Taganana
Distance	14km (8½ miles)
Total Ascent/Descent	1000m (3280ft)
Time	5hrs
Terrain	A rugged coastal path and barranco, followed by steep paths through laurisilva woods.
Refreshment	Bars at Taganana and Afur.
Transport	Regular daily buses serve Taganana from Santa Cruz. Infrequent buses serve Afur and Taborno from La Laguna.
Waymarked route(s)	Route uses PR TF 8.

A cliff coast and a deeply set barranco are linked by a rugged path running from Taganana to Afur. A steep climb into dense laurisilva forest is followed by a descent to Taganana, though it is also possible to climb from Afur to Taborno instead, using Walk 6.

Buses do not enter **Taganana**, but pass on a winding road, so start from the highest bus stop on the edge of the village and walk up a road climbing parallel to the main road. Head for the **church**, where a map-board and signposts stand nearby. Go down the cobbled Camino Cruz de Limera and cross a bridge over the **Barranco de la Iglesia**.

The Camino Cruz de Limera climbs as a steep tarmac road, turning to level cobbles. The narrow Calle Lomo la Chanca is marked on the left, climbing steeply and winding past houses. Cross a

The church in Taganana, looking across the valley to the Roque de Enmedio

Playa de Tamadiste

Beach House

House

Barranco de Tamadiste

▲ *Roque Marrubial*

to Almáciga

TAGANANA

La Bodega de Queque

SF

Afur

Lomo Inchirés

Lomo Centeno

Restaurant

Caserio las Naranjas

Barranco de la Iglesia

N

0   1 km

Las Vueltas

Walk 5

to Santa Cruz

Forestry House

La Cumbre

to Santa Cruz

road and continue up broad then narrow concrete, giving way to a steep, winding stone-paved path. Turn right gently down a road, then branch left up a terrace path, through a tiny gap and gently downhill with a pipe alongside. Continue along a track that levels out at **La Bodega de Queque**. Follow the track down past houses, plots, terraces and palms, and when it steepens it has patchy, broken tarmac on it. Pass a solitary palm tree and the track becomes a broad path leading to a stone-walled **mirador** overlooking the rugged coast.

A narrow path picks a way through a huge, crumbling gully. Further along there are smaller gullies to cross on the slopes of **Roque Marrubial**, where it is hoped that the path will remain in good shape. There are a couple of cultivated slopes and a white shed is prominent for a short while. The path rises and falls, in and out of gullies, crossing a very steep, scrub-covered slope of crumbling conglomerate. A rocky outcrop is seen ahead and the path passes through a gap behind it. The descent starts easily but becomes rough and stony, with a view of **Playa de Tamadiste** and a beach house.

Playa de Tamadiste at the mouth of the Barranco de Tamadiste

Cross the **Barranco de Tamadiste** as marked and turn left to follow a fragmentary path upstream. Cross the bare rock bed of a side-stream and the path begins to climb steeply and ruggedly, passing a big cane thicket below a little **house** adorned with maritime salvage. Keep well below the house and pick a way below terraces. The path climbs and winds, with rocky corners and fine views deep into the barranco. Some short stretches are fenced and the rugged, uneven slopes sometimes feature crude steps. Eventually, cross the barranco and climb crude steps up the other side. The rugged and undulating path is followed by more steps, passing a big stump of rock before crossing a good track. Weave between houses into the tiny village of **Afur**, where there is a little chapel and a bar.

Walk up the paved road from the plaza in Afur and turn right to find a path going up and down a few concrete steps, then up lots of concrete steps beneath a rock overhang to return to the road. Turn right up the road a short way, then right down a path as marked. Keep left at a junction and go down to cross a barranco. A vague and narrow path becomes clearer, but is also steep and rugged, winding up **Lomo Inchirés** to a short, steep concrete track back onto the road. Turn right up the bendy road to pass a **restaurant**.

Turn left as marked up a rugged path to a house. Go behind it and up a concrete path, then keep right up a steep winding path into patchy laurisilva on a ridge. Turn left along a narrow road, then right, picking up the ridge path again. There are occasional views as the path winds up through the laurisilva, sometimes on earthen steps. Level out three times, even dipping slightly, then climb steps and zigzag up a steep slope of dense laurisilva to reach a road and a three-way signpost. ◄ Turn left for Taganana and follow the road to a bus shelter and map-board on a gap around 830m (2725ft) near a **Forestry House** on **La Cumbre**.

Turn left to follow a track to a path junction and signpost. Turn right up steps cut into a deep groove in the bedrock on a slope of laurisilva. The path winds up to

There may be a view of El Teide to the right.

another signpost and turn left to follow the Camino de las Vueltas. This traverses a slope of dense laurisilva and the descent commences with barely any views. Keep ahead at a junction, down a path that becomes a worn gully, but improves on **Las Vueltas**. The trees are tall and the path is obvious, aligning itself to a steep ridge between two barrancos. It winds more and more tightly, then heads left across the **Barranco de la Iglesia**.

The path runs gently across a slope, passing little terraces, then drops beside a forested valley and more terraces. It becomes rough-paved, slippery and uneven, flanked by walls. It winds downhill and has better paving by some houses at **Caserio los Naranjos**. Walk straight ahead as marked up a road, then down past Caserio Portugal. Turn right as marked down the paved 'no through road' of Camino Portugal. This leads down to the bridge over the Barranco de la Iglesia that was used earlier in the day. Turn right to walk up into **Taganana**, then down to the main road to catch a bus.

Emerging from the laurisilva forest with a view down to Taganana

WALK 6

Afur, Taborno and Pico del Inglés

Start	Afur
Finish	Pico del Inglés
Total Ascent	850m (2790ft)
Total Descent	50m (165ft)
Distance	7km (4½ miles)
Time	2hrs 30mins
Terrain	Paved paths and rugged paths, sometimes easy, but sometimes steep, climbing from a barranco to dense laurisilva woods.
Refreshment	Bars at Afur, Taborno and beside the road below Pico del Inglés.
Transport	Infrequent buses serve Afur, Taborno and occasionally Pico del Inglés, from La Laguna.
Waymarked route(s)	Route uses PR TF 2.

A fine paved path, complete with street lights, leaves Afur and climbs towards the village of Taborno, which straddles a narrow ridge. A further ascent through laurisilva forest leads to the summit of Pico del Inglés. This links with Walk 1, offering keen walkers an onward descent towards Santa Cruz.

Start from the plaza in **Afur**, around 200m (655ft), and pass an electricity transformer tower to pick up a concrete path and steps zigzagging down into a barranco. Cross a couple of footbridges and climb an obvious concrete zigzag path, flanked by street lights, up a ridge. ◄ Just as houses are reached at **Lomo Centeno**, fork left and keep zigzagging up the concrete path. A flight of steps leads to the highest houses, but do not go up them. Instead, turn left along a rugged path and climb to a gap high above the houses. Keep left again and keep climbing steps and rocky zigzags. The path contours across a slope, and then stone steps climb past a couple of houses to regain the ridge at **El Frontón**, where a house stands at a road-end. ◄

Fine views unfold as height is gained.

The road can be used to reach Taborno.

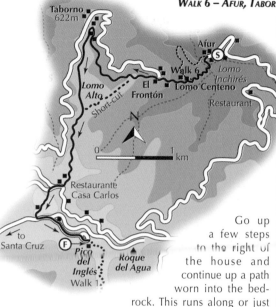

Go up a few steps to the right of the house and continue up a path worn into the bedrock. This runs along or just beside the ridge, with laurisilva woods dropping to the right and incienso-scented scrub dropping to the left. Cross a couple of gaps and reach a path junction.

Following the crest between El Frontón and Taborno, where there is an optional short-cut

Looking across to the village of Taborno, with the Roque de Taborno beyond

A short-cut avoiding Taborno is available by climbing steeply ahead, turning left when a junction with the longer route is reached.

Turn right down into the woods, following the undulating path which generally climbs, in and out of the woods, keeping left at junctions with a couple of other paths. Pass little terraced slopes and join a concrete path leading to a signpost for Pico del Inglés. Either turn left to start climbing, or turn right to visit **Taborno**, its bar restaurant and little chapel, at 622m (2041ft).

A steep, stone-paved path climbs into laurisilva woods, becoming more rugged. Pass a small concrete reservoir. Some parts of the ridge are bare enough to offer good views of the surroundings. There is a rounded hump at **Lomo Alto**, past which the path skirts to reach a gap beyond. Here the short-cut path comes in from the left. Keep straight ahead and down across the slope to another gap. The path climbs and winds onto a higher part of the ridge, with splendid views on either side. Pass another rounded hump and keep climbing through dense woods, passing a small building. Keep climbing past a house and follow a concrete road up to a road bend at the **Restaurante Casa Carlos** (bus services).

Turn right along the road, passing the junction for Taborno, then watch for a path on the left climbing back into laurisilva. On misty days, the woods drip continually, especially the heather trees. The path leads to another road, where a left turn leads to a splendid mirador on **Pico del Inglés**, around 1000m (3280ft). Despite nearby masts there are splendid views of the Anaga peninsula, the urban sprawl of Santa Cruz and La Laguna, with El Teide rising beyond. Gran Canaria lies out to sea. There are occasional buses from here; otherwise follow the road to a junction to pick up other bus services. ▸

Walk 1 can be used to descend towards Santa Cruz.

WALK 7
Cruz del Carmen, Chinamada and Punta del Hidalgo

Start	Cruz del Carmen
Finish	Punta del Hidalgo
Distance	10km (6¼ miles)
Total Ascent	50m (165ft)
Total Descent	1000m (3280ft)
Time	3hrs 30mins
Terrain	Densely forested slopes give way to cultivated slopes and rocky ridges leading down to the coast.
Refreshment	Bars at Cruz del Carmen, Chinamada and Punta del Hidalgo.
Transport	Regular daily buses serve Cruz del Carmen and Punta del Hidalgo from La Laguna.
Waymarked route(s)	Route uses PR TF 10.

This is the easier of two routes descending from Cruz del Carmen to Punta del Hidalgo. After running down slopes of laurisilva, the route reaches the tiny village of Chinamada, noted for its cave houses. A path picks its way across cliffs, exploiting lines of weakness, to continue the descent.

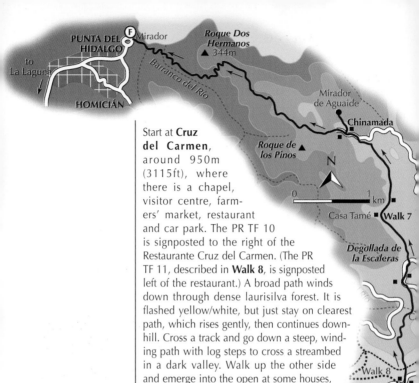

Start at **Cruz del Carmen**, around 950m (3115ft), where there is a chapel, visitor centre, farmers' market, restaurant and car park. The PR TF 10 is signposted to the right of the Restaurante Cruz del Carmen. (The PR TF 11, described in **Walk 8**, is signposted left of the restaurant.) A broad path winds down through dense laurisilva forest. It is flashed yellow/white, but just stay on clearest path, which rises gently, then continues downhill. Cross a track and go down a steep, winding path with log steps to cross a streambed in a dark valley. Walk up the other side and emerge into the open at some houses, **Casas del Río**.

Turn left down a winding grassy track, back into forest and up to a road. Turn left gently down past a house and bus shelter. Turn right at the next houses, along a concrete access track. The idea is to link paths parallel to the road, come down steps beside a covered reservoir and cross the road. Go down steps and a woodland path as marked, to a gap with a pylon, a little cross and a signpost at **Degollada de Las Escaleras**, around 725m (2380ft). ◀

Turning right downhill leads to the village of Las Carboneras, where the road can be followed to Chinamada.

Walk straight ahead across the gap and keep left of a wooded peak. There is a slight ascent with a view down the Barranco del Río, then the path zigzags down a forested slope. Continue along a traverse and keep an eye on yellow/white markers at junctions, reaching a house,

Casa Tamé, where there is a view across the barranco to El Batán. The path runs round the back of the house and descends gently, later undulating and crossing a ridge before dropping on soft, worn bedrock to a road junction. Walk down to the Plaza San Ramón in the tiny village of **Chinamada**, around 610m (2000ft). Guanches lived in caves here until the Conquest. Spanish settlers built houses, but realised that the caves offered better protection from strong winds.

Either take a break at the Restaurante La Cueva or visit the nearby **Mirador de Aguaide** as signposted (1km there and back), or just continue with the walk. Punta del Hidalgo is signposted up a road, then left down a path, and the destination can be seen on the coast far below. Pick a way between cultivation terraces and look down on the **Roque de los Pinos.** ▶ The path rises and falls as it exploits a soft layer in the rock; otherwise the slope is steep and scrub-covered.

Turn a corner for a view of Punta del Hidalgo and of the shattered rocky ridge that still needs to be traversed.

The path runs down a scrub-covered ridge, trodden to bedrock, with increasingly crude rugged steps hammered into it. Swing right to avoid a cliff and cross to an adjacent ridge, traversing up and down, with more steps, exploiting a weak layer. The path runs beneath a severe overhang as it rises and falls, with more rock steps and lots of cardón among the scrub. The descent is rugged and uneven, but always obvious, then drifts easily onto a rocky crest. A fence leads to a remarkably knobbly undercut summit with fine views of the coastal cliffs.

The few Canary pines clinging to the rock are at an unusually low altitude.

Chinamada is notable for its Guanche and post-Conquest caves

A fenced stretch of path passes a remarkably knobbly undercut summit

Zigzag down to a lower gap and another fenced viewpoint, then zigzag down a steep, rugged scrubby slope to outflank the twin peaks of **Roque Dos Hermanos**. The path has been chiselled from unyielding basalt further down, enabling it to reach another sloping weak layer, undercut with caves at first. Later, the path drops steeply, then levels out between a wall and aloes above the bed of the **Barranco del Río**. Zigzag down and cross the barranco, then climb past some derelict buildings to reach a road just outside **Punta del Hidalgo**. Turn left to reach a viewpoint and turning circle, where there is a map-board. A bus stop lies beyond the circle.

WALK 8

*Cruz del Carmen, El Batán and
Punta del Hidalgo*

Start	Cruz del Carmen
Finish	Punta del Hidalgo
Distance	12km (7½ miles)
Total Ascent	250m (820ft)
Total Descent	1200m (3935ft)
Time	4hrs
Terrain	Densely forested slopes give way to cultivated slopes and rocky ridges leading down to the coast. Some paths are steep and rugged.
Refreshment	Bars at Cruz del Carmen, El Batán and Punta del Hidalgo.
Transport	Regular daily buses serve Cruz del Carmen and Punta del Hidalgo from La Laguna. Infrequent buses serve El Batán.
Waymarked route(s)	Route uses PR TF 11.

This is the tougher of two routes from Cruz del Carmen to Punta del Hidalgo. The initial descent through laurisilva forest is straightforward. The walk through the upper Barranco del Río is exciting, but the climb from it is steep, and the Barranco Seco has to be negotiated afterwards.

Start at **Cruz del Carmen**, around 950m (3115ft), where there is a chapel, visitor centre, farmers' market, restaurant and car park. The PR TF 11 is signposted right of the Restaurante Cruz del Carmen. (The PR TF 10, described in **Walk 7**, is signposted left of the restaurant.) Go past a barrier to follow a track flashed yellow/white. A short trail, 'La Hija Cambada', drops to the left, but keep straight ahead and gently uphill through the laurisilva forest. The track runs down and along the well-wooded crest, and all other tracks and paths should be avoided. When a junction is reached on a gap before a building, turn sharp right down a path signposted for El Batán.

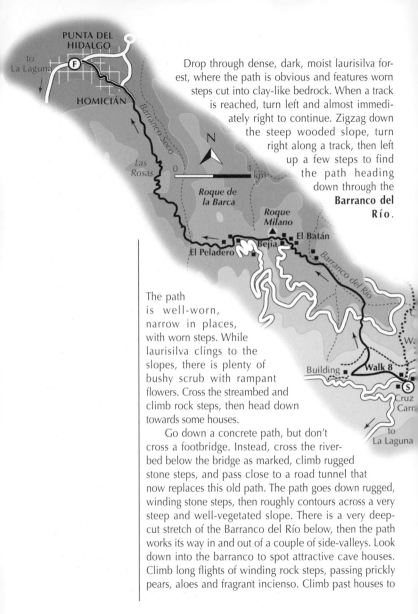

Drop through dense, dark, moist laurisilva forest, where the path is obvious and features worn steps cut into clay-like bedrock. When a track is reached, turn left and almost immediately right to continue. Zigzag down the steep wooded slope, turn right along a track, then left up a few steps to find the path heading down through the **Barranco del Río**.

The path is well-worn, narrow in places, with worn steps. While laurisilva clings to the slopes, there is plenty of bushy scrub with rampant flowers. Cross the streambed and climb rock steps, then head down towards some houses.

Go down a concrete path, but don't cross a footbridge. Instead, cross the riverbed below the bridge as marked, climb rugged stone steps, and pass close to a road tunnel that now replaces this old path. The path goes down rugged, winding stone steps, then roughly contours across a very steep and well-vegetated slope. There is a very deep-cut stretch of the Barranco del Río below, then the path works its way in and out of a couple of side-valleys. Look down into the barranco to spot attractive cave houses. Climb long flights of winding rock steps, passing prickly pears, aloes and fragrant incienso. Climb past houses to

The peculiar outcrop of Roque Milano is passed after leaving El Batán

This little village was a notable centre for growing flax, but now produces fruit and vegetables.

reach a small plaza and chapel in **El Batán** (bar and small information centre). ◄

Climb straight through the village as flashed yellow/ white, up more rock steps. Keep straight ahead until a small picnic site is reached, then turn right to zigzag up more rock steps to reach a gap. The peculiar outcrop of **Roque Milano** looms over the gap, which is cut into thick beds of volcanic ash. There is a fine view beyond of striking peaks.

The path rises and falls across a steep slope, with a handrail alongside for safety. Join a road and turn right down it. Turn right down rock steps and follow a path hacked from rock between houses at **Bejia**. Join a track and follow it down to a road, then turn right to wind down the road. Watch for a marker on the left, revealing a narrow path climbing across the slope. Pass through the bottom of a laurisilva wood, then climb up a slope of incienso to reach a path junction. Turn right and follow the path gently downhill, then go down steep stone steps, almost to the road-end at **El Peladero**.

Curious cave houses deep in the Barranco del Río, below El Batán

Swing left as marked and traverse round a side barranco that feeds into the **Barranco Seco**, dropping into it and climbing from it. Contour gently across a steep rugged slope of shrubs and scrub, heading in and out of another side barranco. Later, pass a stone seat beneath an undercut edge. Go up rock steps and watch for markers to find a way between cultivation terraces. The path runs up and down, in and out, with lush bushy

vegetation in the valleys and low-growing vegetation on arid slopes. The path climbs from a final side barranco, hacked from ash on a slope of prickly pears, calcosas, brambles and lavender. Go up a sweeping zigzag where steps have been hacked from the ash at **Las Rosas**.

Cross a crumbling crest with a view down to the sea, and the path runs down a slope of heather trees, which later thin out and disappear. Wind down into a scrubby side barranco and climb, reaching a pylon where the rising stony path becomes a descending track. The track becomes a road dropping steeply past a few farms on cultivated and scrubby slopes. Go through the suburb of **Homicián** and the road becomes the Camino El Calleon down to **Punta del Hidalgo**. Turn left at the bottom to find a bar and church (more bars, shops, a post office and a bank with an ATM further along).

The upper part of the Barranco Seco, on the way to Bejia and El Peladero

TENO

Garachico is one of a few small settlements that could serve as a base for exploring Teno

The Teno peninsula, in the extreme north-west, is one of the oldest parts of Tenerife. Its rugged coastline features cliffs, its mountains are riven by deep, steep-sided barrancos and the highest parts are covered in laurisilva cloud forest and pines. Small villages are surrounded by slopes that have been terraced for cultivation, and a network of old paths and mule tracks, as well as convoluted roads, link one village with another. Many routes have been signposted and waymarked in recent years. The region is protected as the Parque Rural de Teno, abutting the Reserva Natural Especial El Chinyero.

Six walks are offered on the peninsula, and while each one stands on its own merit as a day walk, some could also be linked together to create a long-distance walk through the peninsula. Walk 14 through the Barranco de Masca needs careful planning. While there are tourist resorts within easy travelling distance of Teno, walkers also have the option of staying at a rural hostel in the mountains near Las Portelas; the Albergue de Bolico, tel. 922-127938, www.alberguebolico.com.

There is an interesting visitor centre at the Finca Los Pedregales, between Buenavista and Las Portelas, tel. 922-447974. It offers plenty of information about walking opportunities in the area. Buses serve the villages on the peninsula from Playa de las Américas, Puerto de la Cruz, Icod de los Vinos and Buenavista del Norte.

WALK 9

Los Poleos and Volcán Chinyero

Start/Finish	Los Poleos
Distance	6.5km (4 miles)
Total Ascent/Descent	150m (490ft)
Time	2hrs
Terrain	Forested slopes of volcanic ash and barren, rugged lava flows.
Refreshment	None.
Transport	Taxis are available in Guía de Isora.
Waymarked route(s)	Route uses PR TF 43.

Volcán Chinyero erupted in 1909, and lies at the heart of the Reserva Natural Especial El Chinyero. A circular trail runs round the volcano, crossing lava flows and ash, while other trails branch from it to reach Santiago del Teide, Erjos, San José de Los Llanos and Garachico.

Motorists approaching the Parque Nacional del Teide from the west pass a sign on the mountain road reading 'Montaña Chinyero' at **Los Poleos**. There is roadside parking and a view of El Teide above forested and bare ash slopes. Walk down an ash track, past a barrier, and across an area quarried for stone. Pass notices for the Parque Natural Corona Forestal and Reserva Natural Especial El Chinyero. Climb a little into pine forest, then the track bends left and right gently downhill.

A path cuts across the track, flashed yellow/white, and this is the PR TF 43, or 'Circular Chinyero' trail. Turn left to follow it gently downhill, winding through the forest and later crossing the track again. Just as the path reaches a blocky lava flow, it swings left to stay on easy ground, reaching the track

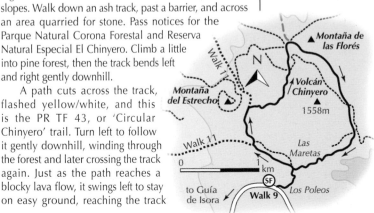

There is a view up the lava flow to El Teide and Pico Viejo.

again at a signpost. Turn right to follow the track easily across a mass of chaotically mangled lava. (The PR TF 43.3 is signposted down to Santiago del Teide.) ◄

The track rises gently from the lava, through more forest, reaching another signpost on the slopes of **Montaña del Estrecho**. Turn right up a few stone steps onto the lava flow. (The PR TF 43.2 is signposted along the track to Los Partidos.) The path picks its way across jagged lava, passing a little plaque commemorating the 100th anniversary of the Volcán Chinyero eruption. Climb past a big upended block of lava, then head down towards pines.

When the path crosses another part of the lava flow, look left to see a level fractured lava crust. The path runs in and out of the forest, winding and undulating, sometimes quite rugged underfoot. Reach a track and signpost and turn right to find a three-way signpost round a bend. Turn right to climb among pines. (The PR TF 43 is signposted to Garachico; it later splits, with the PR TF 43.1 heading to San José de Los Llanos.) The path rises gently among pines, rocks and areas of black volcanic ash. The ash slopes become increasingly bare as the pines thin out on Las Montañitas. Watch for a right turn, and the path climbs across barren ash close to **Volcán Chinyero**.

The ash cone of Volcán Chinyero remains barren while pines struggle to colonise nearby slopes

Turn right along a rising path and climb among sparse pines, later crunching up an ash path, past bare slopes and scattered boulders. Watch for a right turn to reach the highest point on the trail, over 1500m (4920ft), where the cone of Volcán Chinyero looks most bare. Go down into a dip and cross a track; then the path rises from ash onto chunky lava and crosses another track. Climb to a big pine, drop into a dip, then climb across a forested slope with glimpses of the red crater of Volcán Chinyero. Turn right as marked down a very bendy path on a forested ash slope, becoming gentler at the bottom at **Las Maretas**. The track that was used at the start of this walk is reached, and a left turn leads back to the road at **Los Poleos**.

WALK 10
Garachico to San José de los Llanos

Start	Garachico
Finish	San José de los Llanos
Distance	17km (10½ miles)
Total Ascent	1400m (4595ft)
Total Descent	300m (985ft)
Time	6hrs
Terrain	A steep, winding cliff path, followed by steep roads, then gentler tracks and paths up and down forested slopes.
Refreshment	Bars in Garachico, San Juan del Reparo and Los Llanos.
Transport	Regular daily buses serve Garachico from Puerto de la Cruz and Icod de los Vinos. Regular daily buses serve San Juan del Reparo and Los Llanos from Icod de los Vinos.
Waymarked route(s)	Route includes PR TF 43 and PR TF 43.1.

The cliff rising behind Garachico looks impossible to climb, but features a splendid zigzag path. Roads can be followed higher, then forested slopes are threaded by paths and tracks that head in all directions. One line of descent leads to the village of Los Llanos.

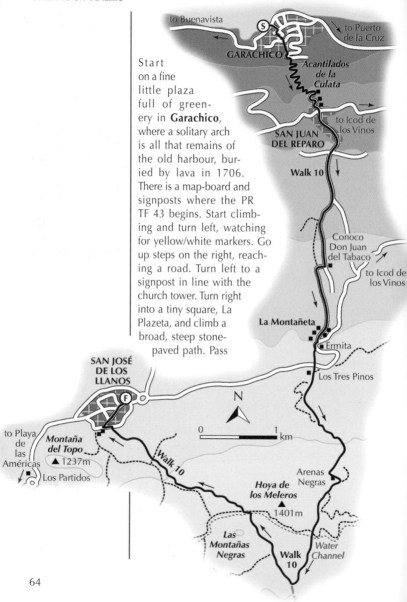

Start on a fine little plaza full of greenery in **Garachico**, where a solitary arch is all that remains of the old harbour, buried by lava in 1706. There is a map-board and signposts where the PR TF 43 begins. Start climbing and turn left, watching for yellow/white markers. Go up steps on the right, reaching a road. Turn left to a signpost in line with the church tower. Turn right into a tiny square, La Plazeta, and climb a broad, steep stone-paved path. Pass

walled terraces and plots, then drift left and go up a few steps onto a road. Turn right up the road, left round a bend, past a barrier gate and black lava to reach a signpost at the edge of the Paisaje Protegido Acantilados de la Culata.

The old harbour at Garachico was destroyed by a lava flow in 1706

Turn right to follow a remarkably bendy path up a steep slope of lava, bare in some places but bearing patchy pines in others. There are splendid views of Garachico, and across the sea to the island of La Palma. Leave the **Acantilados de la Culata** at the top by passing between a mast and a house. Walk up a steep and bendy road, past more houses, always climbing past junctions. ▶ Turn left along a busy road at **San Juan del Reparo**, and right up into a little plaza where there is a church and map-board, around 500m (1640ft).

There is a fine, tall dragon tree to the left.

Look for a signpost on a wall and go along Calle Virgen de las Nieves. Turn left up a remarkably steep street to a junction and a couple of shops. Keep left again and climb steeply further uphill. There is a sudden view stretching from El Teide to the distant Anaga peninsula. Calle El Monte leaves the village where a new

65

road crosses. Climb past old terraces, mostly rampant with bracken and brambles. When a fork in the road is reached, keep right as marked and keep climbing as the laurisilva cover increases. There are fenced-off properties either side, then pines can be seen ahead.

Turn right at a junction opposite **Conoco Don Juan del Tabaco**. There is a slight descent, then turn left and continue climbing, later with houses alongside at **La Montañeta**. Climb straight ahead at a road junction and turn left at another, up to a busy road bend. There is a map-board and signpost, while across the road is the **Ermita San Francisco** and a big picnic area among tall pines.

The route doesn't cross the road, or even touch it, but is marked up the forested slope. Pass a covered reservoir and follow a concrete track up to the main road. Cross over and follow a rugged path, passing pines and regenerating laurisilva. Cross a track at **Los Tres Pinos**, where three pine trunks grow from one root. Walk up the rugged path to a track junction and follow a track running gently uphill. However, watch for the path continuing rather

Clear paths have been blazed through pine forests and across volcanic ash near Arenas Negras

vaguely on the right, dwindling to an ash path marked by tiny cairns. Join a track further uphill and turn right up to the **Área Recreativa Arenas Negras**, where there is a childrens' playground and barbeque sites.

Walk to the top access track to find a map-board and a signpost. Turn right and follow the track up round a bend. A signpost points ahead for Chinyero and the path drops a little, then climbs and winds through forest onto black ash slopes. There is a bare ash cone to the right, and the path is broad, black ash flanked by lines of stones. Walk up to a signpost and cross a track, then climb across a concrete **water channel**, heading in and out of forest, with a blocky lava flow to the right. Continue climbing and look out for the peak of El Teide, before reaching a three-way signpost at a junction of ash paths. ▶

Keep walking ahead to link with Walk 9 around Volcán Chinyero.

Turn right as signposted for the PR TF 43.1 to San José de los Llanos. The path undulates gently, generally downhill, crossing an old track. The path becomes a track heading down past sparse pines onto bare, black ash. There are splendid views from the concrete water channel, taking in El Teide, Pico Viejo and a nearby ash cone, with black slopes and a red top. Looking across the sea, the Roque de los Muchacos can be seen on La Palma.

Cross the water channel and turn sharp left to follow it a short way. The path drops to the right and zig-zags down black ash into the pine forest, flanked by lines of stones all the way, cutting across tracks. There is an understorey of regenerating heather. Pass a little wayside shrine and cross a track, climbing very slightly, then later dropping steeply for a while. The last stretch meanders a lot, but eventually reaches a road on the upper edge of the village of **San José de los Llanos**. Turn left and right and head down to the main road (bars, shops and buses).

WALK 11
Santiago del Teide, Chinyero and Erjos

Start	Santiago del Teide
Finish	Erjos
Distance	14km (8½ miles)
Total Ascent	675m (2215ft)
Total Descent	575m (1885ft)
Time	4hrs 30mins
Terrain	Mostly good tracks and paths up and down bare or forested slopes of volcanic ash or lava.
Refreshment	Bars at Santiago del Teide and Erjos.
Transport	Regular daily buses link Santiago del Teide and Erjos with Puerto de la Cruz and Playa de las Américas.
Waymarked route(s)	Route includes PR TF 43, 43.2 and 43.3.

Santiago del Teide and Erjos are connected by a winding road with a bus service. This route climbs meanders around volcanic cones, crossing rugged lava flows and soft ash slopes, linking with Walk 9 that makes a circuit around the Volcán Chinyero, which erupted in 1909.

Santiago del Teide, at over 900m (2950ft), has a range of good services and facilities, as well as a visitor centre. Take the Icod road, which is an avenue of eucalyptus trees, out of the village. Head right along the road towards **Valle de Arriba**, but follow the road only as far as a white house on the left. Turn right at this point, gently up a walled track. Keep right when the track forks. There is a view of forested ash cones ahead and El Teide far beyond. Pass fields and climb steeply, swinging left towards a derelict concrete building. Before reaching it, turn right up a path flanked by parallel lines of stones. This climbs and winds, crossing a **water channel**.

There are other paths, so keep climbing along the clearest, which broadens and passes almonds,

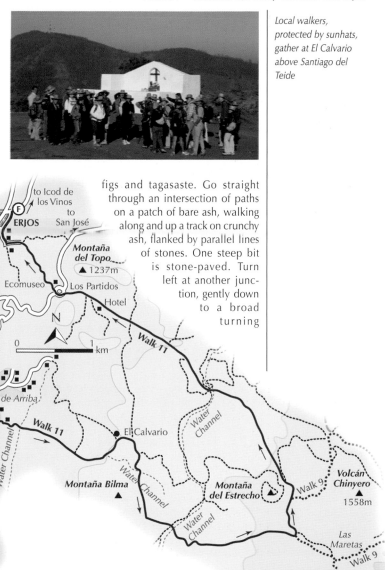

Local walkers, protected by sunhats, gather at El Calvario above Santiago del Teide

figs and tagasaste. Go straight through an intersection of paths on a patch of bare ash, walking along and up a track on crunchy ash, flanked by parallel lines of stones. One steep bit is stone-paved. Turn left at another junction, gently down to a broad turning

Look up the lava flow to its source at Volcán Chinyero, with El Teide and Pico Viejo beyond.

space on the ash beside the white shrine of **El Calvario**, where there is a signpost for the PR TF 43.3.

Keep right at track junctions, climbing gently past figs, with a barren lava flow to the right. Reach another signpost and keep walking ahead. Don't go through a gate on the track, but turn right onto the rugged barren lava flow. A path has been made over it, crossing a broken **water channel**. ◀ Walk down onto an older ash slope at the foot of **Montaña Bilma**, then step back onto the rugged lava and continue downhill. Watch for a sudden left turn down from a path junction, then climb and wander through a bushy area that wasn't covered by lava in 1909.

Cross a track and follow the path over a concrete **water channel**, back onto the barren lava flow. Step down from it and cross another bushy area, turning left uphill at a junction to climb back onto the lava. Keep climbing and the path eventually climbs between the lava flow and a slope of pines. Reach a track and a signpost, where the PR TF 43 'Circular Chinyero' trail is joined, described in **Walk 9**. Turn left to follow the track easily across a mass of chaotically mangled lava, with a view up to El Teide and Pico Viejo. The track rises gently from the lava,

The paths are clearly visible through pine forests on the way to Los Partidos

through forest, reaching another signpost on the slopes of **Montaña del Estrecho**, around 1435m (4710ft).

Keep straight ahead as signposted for Los Partidos, along and down the track, then down a path flanked by stones on the right. Cross the track further down and continue gently down through the forest. The broad path narrows and becomes a black ash path flanked by stones. Follow this and link with a vague, undulating track. Avoid turning down to the left at vague junctions, but pick up and follow the black ash path flanked by stones again. This winds and undulates, but generally heads downhill. Slopes and hummocks of ash are strewn with boulders and blocky lava. Cross a track and continue down the path through the forest.

Cross a concrete **water channel**, cross a track and use a short path just to clip a bend on the track. Cross the track near a junction and go down a rougher, stonier stretch of path. There are several tight bends on a steep and rocky slope, then another gentle ash path. The track is seen from time to time on the descent and the path joins it to continue down through the forest. Reach a signposted track junction at the edge of the forest, and keep straight ahead. A huge area of tagasaste has been burnt on either side of the track.

Go straight through a signposted intersection of tracks and leave the Reserva Natural Especial El Chinyero. There is a **hotel** and restaurant to the left later, otherwise continue down past forest to reach a roundabout and a huge pine, Pino del Loro, at **Los Partidos**. Across the roundabout is access to the **Ecomuseo de El Tanque**. Head that way and keep left of the site. Keep left of a large *era*, or circular threshing floor, and right of another *era*.

Go down a track that gives way to an increasingly rough and rocky path past bushy scrub. Turn right and the path rises a little among heather trees, then drops between overgrown brambly terraces. It becomes broader and heads down to a road and signpost. Turn left along the road and right at a house. Walk down past more houses to a plaza, main road, bus shelters and a nearby bar in **Erjos**, around 1000m (3280ft). ▶

Walks 12 and 13 start here.

71

WALK 12

Erjos to Punta de Teno

Start	Erjos
Finish	Punta de Teno
Distance	20km (12½ miles)
Total Ascent	800m (2625ft)
Total Descent	1700m (5580ft)
Time	7hrs
Terrain	Mostly good tracks and paths, on forested, scrub-covered or rocky slopes. Some paths are steep and rugged.
Refreshment	Bars at Erjos and Teno Alto.
Transport	Regular daily buses serve Erjos from Puerto de la Cruz and Playa de las Américas. A pick-up must be arranged at Punta de Teno.
Waymarked route(s)	Route uses PR TF 51.

The Teno peninsula features a mountainous crest, or *cumbre*, blessed with good paths. These can be linked for a high-level romp over the mountains linking the villages of Erjos and Teno Alto. A steep descent from the mountains allows the coast to be reached at Punta de Teno.

Start at the plaza in **Erjos**, around 1000m (3280ft), and cross the road to go down steps beside a little church. There are signposts across the road from the church, and more signposts just down the road. Turn left down a path, which levels out at yet another signpost. Keep ahead, as signposted for the PR TF 51 to Punta de Teno. ◄ The path is deep in the bottom of a valley that can carry water. However, it is like a track and allows access to adjacent fields. Cross a concrete bridge and a bend on a broad track at the same time. Continue along the track as signposted, rising gently to join another track. Walk ahead and quickly pick up a path to another track. Pass between **flooded quarries** and turn right as signposted between more flooded quarries.

The route follows a track perched on a ridge between quarries, leading up to a signpost where a path heads off

Walk 13 turns right for Las Portelas.

to the left. The way ahead is rather like a rugged gully, but it gets easier underfoot, winding up a slope of burnt tree heather struggling to regenerate. Reach a narrow road that serves a mast on the pine-forested hill of **Cruz de Gala**. Cross over the road and go down a track, contouring across a slope, enjoying views of El Teide, Pico Viejo and Santiago del Teide. The track later rises and ends suddenly, so climb and wind up a path on bare rock, passing sparse scrub, reaching a gap at **Degollada de la Mesa**, at 1247m (4091ft).

Follow the path across the gap as marked, not down the other side, but drifting right and cutting

A mast and fire tower on Cruz de Gala are notable landmarks at the start of the walk

Map continues on page 75

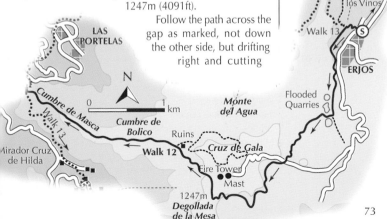

down across slopes below a **fire tower**. The way is often on bare rock, but there is some cistus, as well as heather trees and tagasaste. Fork left at a path junction as marked, and the trees become dense, with the heather being particularly stout. Reach a track and some ruined buildings on a gap on the **Cumbre de Bolico**. Turn left as signposted for Punta de Teno.

Pass between the ruins and an *era*, or circular threshing floor, to follow the path through tagasaste and heather. Later, this descends a steep worn groove through laurisilva, making a traverse across the slope. There are no views until a rocky crest is gained on the **Cumbre de Masca**. The path is rugged down to a gap, then it climbs over a hump, leaves the crest and makes another downward traverse across a slope of laurisilva. Cross another gap, then move left onto the more arid side of the ridge. Continue a downward traverse past prickly pears, cistus, tabaibal and verode. Turn a rocky corner to find a slope of aloes, and follow the rugged crest down to a gap at 886m (2970ft). ◄

Walk 13 crosses here, between Las Portelas and Masca.

Keep walking ahead, alongside the ridge as signposted for Punta de Teno. The path descends to a gap, then switches from side to side on the ridge, in and out of laurisilva, but mostly across slopes of mixed scrub on the **Cumbre del Carrizal**. Go down chunky steps to land on an awkward road bend. Cross the road to find information about the view from this prominent gap, at 815m (2675ft) (bus service).

Follow an easy path along a crest scented with incienso. A steep and rugged climb continues, often trodden to bare rock, zigzagging up a scrubby slope and passing through laurisilva. The path is easier at that point, then stone steps zigzag further uphill and another easier stretch stays below the rocky ridge. Stone steps climb higher and the path cuts across a slope dotted with aloes, missing

the highest point. To climb to the summit, watch for a less well-trodden path up to the right from a stone seat. This is rugged and squeezes through heather scrub to reach a trig point on **Baracán**, at 1003m (3291ft).

The main path traverses a slope of scrub and aloes, climbing past a couple of tall prickly pears, passing cistus to get back onto the crest. The path is remarkably easy along the crest, where laurisilva grows. Head down, left of the crest, across a slope of cistus and big boulders, with views of rugged barrancos falling to the sea. Go through laurisilva, gently down across a slope, onto a worn red gap. Go down steps to a concrete road serving a circular green **reservoir**. Turn right along the concrete road, go down a tarmac road past buildings, passing heather trees on the way down to the tiny village of **Teno Alto**, around 800m (2625ft), where there are a couple of bars, a church and a map-board.

Follow a road out of the village, signposted for Punta de Teno. This descends across a grassy slope and rises to a signpost. Continue ahead, gently down a track, until a junction is reached at a signpost. Turn sharp right further downhill, across grassy slopes on red pumice bedrock. Cross a road as signposted and continue down a path. Avoid the road and stay on a rough and rocky path along the brow of the **Barranco de las Cuevas**, fringed by aloes and tabaibal.

Join the road to pass a little house, then follow the rugged path again, passing masses of prickly pears along one stretch. Later, another stretch runs into prickly pears before another house. Turn left down a rugged path, winding down into the barranco. Cross over and climb a grassy track, becoming concrete near the top, then cross a rise below **Los Partidos** and go down through a gate. The track later finishes, overlooking cultivation tents and

A red rock outcrop overlooks cultivation tents at Teno Baja towards the end of the walk

wind turbines. Descend as marked from a stone wind-break, taking care as the path is very rocky and stony and its zigzags cannot be hurried. Scrub on the slope includes cardón, tabaibal, verode, aulaga, cornical and asphodel. Land on a road at **Teno Bajo**, beside a map-board and signpost.

Turn left and follow the road straight towards **Punta de Teno**. There are lots of prickly pears along the way, and the road goes out onto a rugged point of crumbling pumice, battered by the sea. There is no access to the lighthouse, **Faro de Teno**, but there are splendid views along the cliffs towards the mouth of the Barranco de Masca. ▶

There is no bus service and a pick-up must be arranged.

WALK 13
Erjos, Las Portelas and Masca

Start	Erjos
Distance	16km (10 miles)
Finish	Masca
Total Ascent	300m (985ft)
Total Descent	590m (1935ft)
Time	5hrs
Terrain	A gentle and easy forest track from village to village, followed by a rugged ascent and descent.
Refreshment	Bars at Erjos, Las Portelas and Masca.
Transport	Regular daily buses serve Erjos from Puerto de la Cruz and Playa de las Américas. Daily buses serve Las Portelas and Masca from Buenavista and Santiago del Teide.
Waymarked route(s)	Route uses PR TF 52 and PR TF 59.

A gentle, but remarkably bendy track runs between the villages of Erjos and Las Portelas, across steep slopes of laurisilva forest on Monte del Agua. Another path can be followed over the Cumbre de Masca onto rugged arid slopes, descending to the popular little village of Masca.

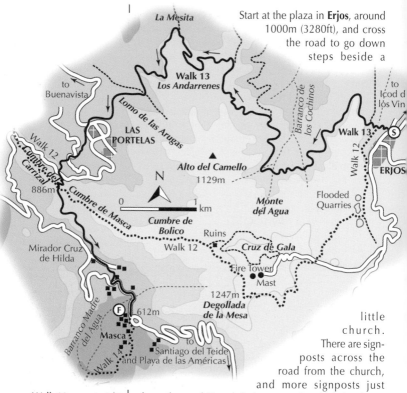

Start at the plaza in **Erjos**, around 1000m (3280ft), and cross the road to go down steps beside a little church. There are signposts across the road from the church, and more signposts just down the road. Turn left down a path, which levels out at yet another signpost. Turn right as signposted for the PR TF 52/54 to Las Portelas. ◀

Walk 12 runs straight ahead for Punta de Teno.

The path climbs, flanked by gorse and brambles, to a couple of masts and a signpost beside a track. Walk straight ahead along the track, entering the Parque Rural Teno. Simply follow the bendy track gently down through tall laurisilva forest, across the slopes of **Monte del Agua** and around the head of the **Barranco de los Cochinos**, with no views for a long time until a signpost and mapboard are reached at a junction. Keep left, in effect straight ahead along the main track, at this junction and

78

at two more junctions further along, while turning round apparently endless bends. Signposts indicate the PR TF 52 for Las Portelas. Eventually the laurisilva gives way to slopes of tangled scrub and another junction is reached. Keep straight ahead and follow the track down to a road and houses, reaching a bus shelter at the bottom end of **Las Portelas**, around 630m (2070ft). ▶

There are bars at the top of the village.

Cross the road to study the signposts and a map-board at a road junction, and follow the PR TF 59 for Masca, up the gentle Calle de Fuera. The road later turns left and steepens, so keep straight ahead along a grassy track instead. This becomes a concrete track down into a barranco. Go down the grassy bed of the barranco, then turn left up a steep and narrow path, joining a road at a signpost. Go up the road, round a couple of bends on a scrub-covered slope, climbing from another signpost to reach a higher main road.

A signpost at a path intersection on a gap at 886m (2970ft) where Walk 12 and Walk 13 cross

Turn left along the road, only for a short way, then turn right up a path as marked. This climbs through laurisilva and reaches a bare and rocky patch on the **Cumbre de Masca**, where there is a signpost, at 886m (2970ft). Walk 12 crosses here, from Erjos to Punta de Teno. Cross the ridge and contour past prickly pears and aloes. Turn a rocky corner and traverse past bushy broom. The path descends gradually to the road at the **Mirador Cruz de Hilda**, where there is a cafetería beneath the viewpoint.

There is no need to follow the bendy road, which carries a lot of traffic. Instead, go down an old road as marked, until a broad path slices down

The little village of Masca (also the start of Walk 14) is well worth exploring

Walk 14 down the Barranco de Masca starts here.

to the right, signposted for Masca. Go down past a water store and wind down terrace paths as marked. A stone-paved track reaches the road again at a huddle of houses. Turn left down the bendy road to reach the busy little village of **Masca**, at 612m (2008ft), which is well worth exploring while waiting for a bus. ◄

WALK 14

Barranco de Masca

Start	Masca
Finish	Playa de Masca
Distance	4km (2½ miles) one way
Total Descent	610m (2000ft)
Time	2hrs one way
Terrain	A long, steep, rough and rocky descent, and if no ferry is available, the whole route has to be reversed.
Refreshment	Bars at Masca.
Transport	Daily buses serve Masca from Buenavista and Santiago del Teide. Ferries from Playa de Masca to Los Gigantes must be booked in advance, tel. 922-861918.
Note	The Barranco de Masca may one day feature controlled access, similar to the Barranco del Infierno, in which case it would be necessary to book your visit in advance. At the time of writing, access was still free.

The deep and rugged Barranco de Masca is very popular, but walking through it requires care. Many people walk down to the mouth of the barranco to be collected by ferry, while others retrace their steps. Remember that climbing back up to Masca is much more difficult than the descent.

Start at the busy little village of **Masca**, at 612m (2008ft). Walk down a stone-paved path, past the plaza, with its huge tree and chapel, past souvenir stalls and bar restaurants, towards the Bar Blanky. Turn left before the bar, down a steep and rugged path with some wooden steps. Old terraces sprout palms, aloes, broom, tabaibal and other plants. A huge rock towers over the right-hand side of the **Barranco de Masca**, and the path is easy for a while, then squeezes between huge boulders derived from a thick layer of boulder agglomerate.

Cross a footbridge and climb a little, then follow narrow, rocky and slightly exposed paths. Pass some

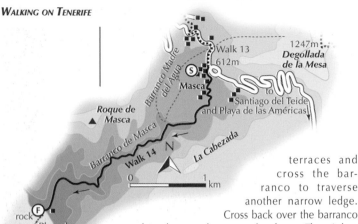

terraces and cross the barranco to traverse another narrow ledge. Cross back over the barranco where there are dense growths of cane. There is low headroom beneath a big boulder, then a rocky rib with pools alongside leads down to a concrete dam. The other barranco joining at this point is the **Barranco Madre del Agua**.

Weave about on the broad and bouldery bed and cross to the right to avoid an enormous boulder-choke. There is only one path down from here, either on the bed of the barranco or just to one side. The rock walls are sheer, even overhanging, often with no vegetation. The bed of the barranco is either stony or bouldery, sometimes thick with vegetation, and there might be a trickle of water. Keep winding down through the narrow gorge, where the path is occasionally buttressed on one side. Look out for a rock arch like a flying buttress up to the left. The barranco narrows even further and leads some to believe it reaches a dead-end! However, a bouldery ramp leads up and across a steep and rocky slope. ◄

If planning to climb back later, be sure to remember this feature.

Further down the barranco, on the left-hand side, there is a short scramble along a rocky rib. Apart from this, keep weaving from side to side and admire the deep, green rock pools and occasional trickles of water. A stretch of path on the right-hand side gives way to a stretch of path on the left. Listen carefully and the sea may be audible. Climb a little, then zigzag down a few terraces. After another little climb, a tiny portion of the sea can be glimpsed. More

The Barranco de Masca has sheer rock walls in many places and there is only one way down through it

light enters the barranco, but there are still a couple of little scrambles to be made past dry waterfalls either side of a huge boulder jammed overhead.

The bouldery barranco continues down to the sea at **Playa de Masca**, where there are tamarisk bushes and other clumps of vegetation. A little house crouches at the base of a cliff and there may be roving packs of cats looking for food handouts! A concrete walkway leads to a solitary rock, which is popular with swimmers when sea conditions allow. ◄

Looking across the sea, the island of La Gomera can be seen.

If a pick-up has been arranged by ferry, then be sure to arrive on time. Pick-ups for pre-booked passengers are usually at 1330, 1530 and 1630. If no ferry has been booked, or if they aren't available at the time of your visit, then the hardest part of the trip is yet to come. The climb back up through the barranco, returning to **Masca**, is much, much more difficult than the descent, especially if it is made in the hottest part of the day.

A little mirador at Masca allows a view into the upper part of the Barranco de Masca

ARONA/GUÍA

Steep and rugged hills, such as Roque del Conde (left), rise above the resort of Los Cristianos

The southern part of Tenerife has a rugged coastline dotted with bustling holiday resorts. Rising steeply inland are arid, degraded cultivation terraces, giving way to deep, steep-sided barrancos and rugged low mountains. Away from the resorts, a fine network of paths and tracks link the villages of Arona, Vilaflor, La Escalona, Adeje and Guía de Isora. Many routes have been signposted and waymarked in recent years. The higher parts are dominated by pine forest, protected as the Parque Natural de Corona Forestal. Further downhill are several other protected areas.

Seven walks are offered in this area, and while each one stands on its own merit as a day walk, some of them also link with the long-distance GR 131. Walk 15 through the Barranco del Infierno has been closed for some time, but check for the current situation, tel. 922-782885, www.barrancodelinfierno.es.

While the tourist resorts lie within easy travelling distance, many walkers would prefer to lodge in the quieter mountain villages, and the highest of these, indeed the highest village in the Canary Islands, is Vilaflor. Bear in mind that some routes also approach Vilaflor from the Parque Nacional del Teide. Buses serve walks in this area from Playa de las Américas, Los Cristianos, Guía de Isora and Granadilla.

WALK 15

Barranco del Infierno

Start/Finish	Adeje
Distance	7km (4½ miles) there and back
Total Ascent/Descent	300m (985ft)
Time	3hrs
Terrain	Steep road to the barranco entrance, then a path across exceptionally rugged slopes.
Refreshment	Bars in Adeje.
Transport	Regular daily buses serve Adeje from Los Cristianos, Playa de las Américas, Guía de Isora and Los Gigantes.

The walk into the Barranco del Infierno was one of the most popular on Tenerife. Access became strictly controlled and had to be pre-booked. Contact information was provided, tel. 922-782885, www.barrancodelinfierno.com, but in recent years the gate was closed, apparently for 'safety reasons'.

While there is no doubt that rocks could come crashing into the narrow head of the barranco at any time, some walkers are willing to by-pass the locked gate and enjoy the walk regardless. As they forge onwards, the steep slopes support lush vegetation, as the barranco is quite well-watered. In the end, sheer rock walls often feature a waterfall and plunge pool, and steps need to be retraced afterwards. This route is retained in this guidebook in case the barranco should re-open.

The toughest part of this walk is reaching the entrance to the barranco by road! Start from the bus stops in the lower part of **Adeje** and walk up through town. Turn left at the church to walk on the level, then turn right as signposted for the barranco, up the steep Calle de Molinos. The last part of this road is the steepest, and is stone-paved beside the Bar Restaurante Otelo. The entrance to the **Barranco del Infierno** is just above, on the right. A paved mirador offers views along the barranco, taking in nearby towers of rock and the more distant Roque del Conde.

Currently, a locked gate bars access, but some walkers by-pass it, then follow an easy path across a steep and

A waterfall spills into a deep gorge and there is no further access for walkers

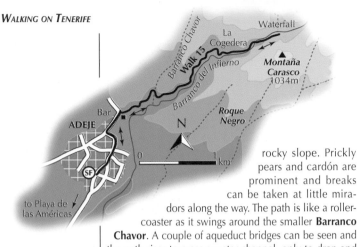

rocky slope. Prickly pears and cardón are prominent and breaks can be taken at little miradors along the way. The path is like a rollercoaster as it swings around the smaller **Barranco Chavor**. A couple of aqueduct bridges can be seen and the path rises to cross a water channel, only to drop and cross it again on its way down to the bed of the **Barranco del Infierno**.

The path crosses and re-crosses the barranco and, depending on the amount of water present, footbridges may or may not be needed. Pass the site of a small dam at **La Cogedera** and note how the vegetation becomes more dense and luxuriant. At a higher level several chestnut trees flourish. Later, the rock walls rise sheer, and even overhang, so the vegetation cover finishes as hardly any sunlight can penetrate. A cave-like recess with only a tiny bit of sky overhead features a slender **waterfall** cascading into a broad pool.

This is as far as you can walk, so take a break and enjoy the coolness of the place. When the time comes to leave, simply retrace your steps back through the barranco to return to **Adeje**.

WALK 16
Arona and Roque del Conde

Start/Finish	Plaza Cristo de la Salud, Arona
Distance	7km (4½ miles) there and back
Total Ascent/Descent	500m (1640ft)
Time	3hrs
Terrain	A well-trodden path on steep, rocky, scrub-covered slopes.
Refreshment	Bars in Arona.
Transport	Regular daily buses serve Arona and from Los Cristianos and Vilafor.

Despite the formidable appearance of the Roque del Conde, which towers above the resorts of Los Cristianos and Playa de las Américas, there is a popular path from Arona to the summit. The lower slopes and the summit plateau were terraced and formerly supported cereal crops.

The village of **Arona** has a good range of services. Start on the Plaza Cristo de la Salud, around 630m (2065ft). There is a map-board behind the church and the walk starts by following a road, Calle San Carlos Borromeo, up out of town. Cross the main road and follow a road signposted for Roque del Conde. Climb past a house, La Casa del Pintor, around 650m (2130ft) at **Vento**, and walk downhill. Turn left down Calle Vento, then right between houses, where a stub of tarmac road and a track give way to stone steps down into a barranco.

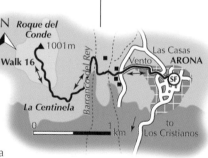

Climb uphill and cross a rocky scrubby slope featuring prickly pears, tabaibal, verode, cardón, lavender and rushes. ▶ Keep straight ahead at a path junction and cross

The long-distance GR 131, Walk 41, turns right off this path.

89

Climbing from the Barranco del Rey to Roque del Conde, with Roque Imoque in the distance

a concrete water channel and a pipe. The path enters a Reserva Natural Especial as it drops into the **Barranco del Rey**. Climb stone steps, passing a ruined farmhouse and two circular *eras*, or threshing floors. Climb past old cultivation terraces; cardón becomes prominent as the path climbs to the rugged shoulder of **La Centinela**, at 775m (2543ft). Enjoy the fine views before continuing along a more rugged stretch.

The path makes a rough traverse across a steep, rocky scrubby slope, then winds uphill. Reach a gentle slope of old cultivation terraces and keep climbing to reach the summit trig point on **Roque del Conde** at 1001m (3284ft). The highest parts are covered in asphodel and the extensive views encompass not only nearby resorts but also Adeje, Barranco del Infierno, Masca, El Teide, Barranco del Rey, La Escalona and the Corona Forestal. Across the sea lie Gran Canaria, El Hierro, La Gomera and La Palma.

A network of easy paths wander around the highest old cultivation terraces; otherwise the whole summit is surrounded by cliffs and the only safe way back to **Arona** is to retrace your steps.

WALK 17
Arona and Roque Imoque

Start/Finish	Plaza Cristo de la Salud, Arona
Distance	10km (6¼ miles)
Total Ascent/Descent	450m (1475ft)
Time	3hrs 30mins
Terrain	Well-trodden paths on steep, rocky, scrub-covered slopes.
Refreshment	Bars in Arona. Bar at El Refugio.
Transport	Regular daily buses serve Arona and from Los Cristianos and Vilafor.

The Roque Imoque is a prominent and striking peak dominating the countryside around Arona, Ifonche and La Escalona. Paths make an easy circuit around it, but the summit is gained only by hands-on scrambling. The approach from Arona follows the first stage of the long-distance GR 131.

The village of **Arona** has a good range of services. Start on the Plaza Cristo de la Salud, around 630m (2065ft). There is a map-board behind the church and the walk starts by following a road, Calle San Carlos Borromeo, up out of town. Cross the main road and follow a road signposted for Roque del Conde. Climb past a house, La Casa del Pintor, around 650m (2130ft) at **Vento**, and walk downhill. Turn left down Calle Vento, then right between houses, where a stub of tarmac road and a track give way to stone steps down into a barranco.

Climb uphill and cross a rocky, scrubby slope featuring prickly pears, tabaibal, verode, cardón, lavender and rushes. ▶ Watch for a path climbing on the right, flanked by stones, crossing a concrete water channel and a pipe. The path continues to be flanked by stones, with a fenced edge where it overlooks the **Barranco del Rey**. Keep well to the left of a building and drop easily into the barranco before reaching a ruin at **Ancón**.

Walk 16 continues straight ahead for Roque del Conde.

There is a view over the edge to Adeje, with the islands of La Gomera and La Palma can be seen across the sea.

Climb steps and follow an easy path flanked by stones and scrub. Keep left of a ruined building and a circular *era*, or threshing floor, and note a well down to the left. The path climbs and drifts left, winding up through a valley to reach a gap, **Degollada de los Frailes**, below Roque del Conde. ◄

Turn right and follow a path hacked from ash and pumice on the slopes of Montaña de Suárez. The path keeps below the summit, crossing a gentle gap near **Casa de Suárez**, where there is a stone water channel and an *era*. Climb again towards the prominent tower-like **Roque Imoque**. The path keeps well below the summit, with a fenced edge as it reaches a gap at the head of **Barranco de Fañabe**. A splendid *era* sits on the gap, and there is an option to climb Roque Imoque.

Ascent of Roque Imoque

Turn right on reaching the gap and follow a path up a steep and scrubby ridge. Looking uphill a rocky peak is

The path reaches a gap and a circular era, or threshing floor, beneath Roque Imoque

*Take care where the
path gets tangled
among old water
channels on the
descent to Arona*

seen and this can be climbed only by using hands, and
only by those with a good head for heights. The summit
of Roque Imoque stands at 1112m (3648m) and it might
still bear a flag on a tall pole. Although less than 1km
(½ mile) there and back, allow an hour for a summit bid
from the gap.

To omit the climb and walk back to Arona, follow a gritty
path down from the *era*, keeping right of a ruined building. The path drops into the **Barranco del Rey**, but look
across it to spot a building, which is where you should
emerge after following a vague path up the other side.
Turn right along a track and follow it to another building
in a huddle of pines. This is **El Refugio**, a bar offering a
fine view southwards.

Walk down a broad and rugged path from the bar, passing a couple more houses before a steep and narrow path continues down a scrubby slope. Head for a little concrete reservoir and follow a track down past the ruins of **Casa del Topo**. Just below the house, watch out for a path branching left from the track. Continue down a rugged, scrubby slope towards another **reservoir**, taking care where the path gets tangled among old water channels and pipes. Just below the reservoir dam is a track and a signpost.

There are two possible endings. The quicker is to turn left and follow the track easily across the Barranco del Ancón to reach the road beside the Restaurante La Granja. Turn right down the road to pass **Las Casas**, and later turn left back into **Arona**.

For the longer route, turn right along the track and follow a path past the ruined **Ancón**. The path winds down into a barranco and climbs the other side. When it reaches a junction, turn left and retrace the earlier steps of the day back to **Vento** and along the road to **Arona**.

WALK 18
La Escalona, Ifonche and Adeje

Start	La Escalona
Alternative Start	Adeje
Finish	Adeje
Distance	16km (10 miles)
Total Ascent	400m (1310ft)
Total Descent	1100m (3610ft)
Time	5hrs
Terrain	After an initial road-walk, paths wind and undulate across a forested slope. There is a rugged descent on a scrub-covered slope.
Refreshment	Bars in La Escalona. Bar at Ifonche. Bars in Adeje.
Transport	Regular daily buses serve La Escalona from Los Cristianos and Vilaflor, while Adeje is served from Los Cristianos, Playa de las Américas, Guía de Isora and Los Gigantes.

This linear route uses a road from La Escalona to Ifonche, then follows tracks and paths across forested slopes. A steep and rugged descent leads to Adeje, passing the entrance to the Barranco del Infierno (Walk 15). There are plenty of bus services to and from the start and finish. An alternative ascent from Adeje is also described.

Start at the bus stop at the lower end of **La Escalona**, around 1000m (3280ft), where a road is signposted uphill for Ifonche. If you can, arrange a lift along this road to save 3km (2 miles) and one hour's walking. The road climbs and descends past cultivated plots, a couple of bars and the **Ermita de Ifonche**. The road is forested as it crosses Barranco del Rey, then climbs to a crossroads at the Bar Restaurant El Dornajo in Ifonche. ◄

The GR 131, Walk 41, crosses here.

Keep straight ahead and follow the road across a dip, then turn right along a track signposted for the Barranco del Infierno. Turn left along a rocky, well-worn path. Cross a forested rise and walk down past old terraces. Walk a few paces up a track to a junction. It is worth turning left and keeping left of a house called **Benitez**, to reach a circular *era*, or threshing floor. There is a splendid view down into the rock-walled **Barranco del Infierno**. Double back to the path/track junction and turn left uphill to continue. ◄

The alternative ascent from Adeje joins here.

Stay on the clearest path up the forested slope, undulating and watching for green/white paint flashes or little cairns where the path is vague. The path winds uphill before dropping to cross the **Barranco de la Fuente**. Climb steeply up the other side, then the path winds and undulates across gentler valleys and crests in the forest. The forest floor is often bare, but sometimes supports cistus and rock rose. Don't worry about the destination 'Taucho' painted on rocks around **Calderón**, but keep following the clearest marked path ahead.

A fork is reached where a path to the left might be blocked by stones, while a paint-marked path climbs gently right. Either path will do, but the one to the

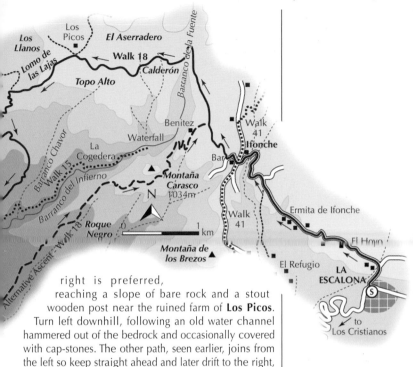

right is preferred,
reaching a slope of bare rock and a stout
wooden post near the ruined farm of **Los Picos**.
Turn left downhill, following an old water channel
hammered out of the bedrock and occasionally covered
with cap-stones. The other path, seen earlier, joins from
the left so keep straight ahead and later drift to the right,
away from the old water channel. A clear path passes
a few pines on the scrubby crest of **Lomo de las Lajas**.
Later, a path comes in from the right, from Taucho. Swing
left through a rock cutting at **Roque de las Lajas** for a
view down to Adeje.

The path zigzags downhill, clearly and obviously,
stone-paved in places, but rugged underfoot so it cannot be hurried. The steep slope bears a few pines but it
is otherwise covered in tabaibal, verode, cistus, prickly
pears, cardón and cornical. Rugged pumice is crossed on
the lower slopes and the path heads towards a couple
of prominent masts. Join a road at the entrance to the
Barranco del Infierno and Bar Restaurante Otelo. Walk
straight down the steep Calle de Molinos, turning left at

97

A steep, stone-paved path descends from Roque de las Lajas to Adeje

the bottom to walk on the level to a church. Turn right and walk down through the centre of **Adeje** to find bus stops towards the bottom of town.

Alternative Ascent from Adeje

An alternative ascent is possible from **Adeje**, starting at the bottom of town, crossing the **Barranco del Infierno**. As the path climbs it becomes steep and narrow in places, following an old, sometimes crumbling, stone water channel. Although marked with green/white flashes of paint, it is really only for walkers willing to scramble on rocky slopes, providing they also have a good head for heights. The route crosses the flank of **Montaña Carasco** and crosses a crumbling gap. It traverses a lush vegetated slope beneath a cliff then becomes stone-paved as it zig-zags up to a crest of pines and cistus. Turn left uphill to reach a circular *era* near **Benitez**, then continue with the rest of the route back round to **Adeje**.

WALK 19
Vilaflor and Montaña de la Vica

Start/Finish	Bus stop at Vilaflor
Distance	10km (6¼ miles)
Total Ascent/Descent	350m (1150ft)
Time	3hrs
Terrain	Roads, tracks and mountain paths, running across cultivated and forested slopes.
Refreshment	Bars in Vilaflor.
Transport	Regular daily buses serve Vilaflor from Los Cristianos and Granadilla.
Waymarked route(s)	Route uses GR 131.

This circular walk from the mountain village of Vilaflor makes use of a forest track to reach Montaña de los Pinos. It links with the course of the long-distance GR 131, which is followed past Montaña de la Vica and Montaña Ciruelita to return to Vilaflor.

Start from the bus stop at the lower end of **Vilaflor**, around 1380m (4530ft), and walk down the road sign-posted for Las Américas. Just after the Km17 marker, turn right up a clear, walled track, passing terraces of vines. Cross a crest over 1400m (4595ft), where the island of La Gomera can be seen in the distance across the sea. Walk down past terraces into thickets of tagasaste. The track rises and falls to reach **Finca Tabaluga**.

A clear track climbs from Vilaflor, rising and falling on its way to the Finca Tabaluga

Turn left just before the building, walking down into pine forest mixed with tagasaste, cistus and rock rose. The track climbs from the **Barranco de Abejera**. Turn left at a junction and head down into another barranco. Climb again and drop a little to cross another small barranco. Climb past a cutting in black ash, cross over a crest at 1394m (4573ft), and head down between a few little terraces near **Montaña de los Pinos**.

When a mass of pipes are seen on the right, pass them and turn right up a narrow path, which is also the route of the long-distance GR 131 (Walk 41). This climbs and zigzags up a forested slope of red pumice. The gradient eases and the path crosses a gentle gap, over 1500m (4920ft) at the back of **Montaña de la Vica**. The ground is very rocky but the path is easy, undulating and winding, always obvious ahead. A couple of spur paths lead left towards circular enclosures with low walls. The path crosses a bouldery streambed close to where the stream leaps over a cliff into the Barranco de Abejera.

The church of San Pedro occupies a prominent position in the village of Vilaflor

Follow the path onwards and uphill, around a big rocky bluff. The highest point of the day's walk is gained, around 1600m (5250ft). A water pipe runs beside the path, which drops gently towards a covered **reservoir**. Walk down the rugged access track and keep left at a junction, down through forest, levelling out to pass through a cultivated area. Another short stretch through forest leads to a road-end between a football pitch and **Hotel Vill Alba**.

Pass the hotel and keep left at a fork in the road. The Ermita San Roque has a small plaza offering a fine view of Vilaflor. Walk down a stone-paved path and steps beside the road. Cross the main road and follow Calle Los Molinos down into **Vilaflor**, reaching the church of San Pedro and its plaza, around 1465m (4805ft). Continue down through the village to return to the bus stop.

WALK 20
Vilaflor and the Paisaje Lunar

Distance	13km (8 miles)
Start/Finish	Iglesia de San Pedro, Vilaflor
Total Ascent/Descent	500m (1640ft)
Time	5hrs
Terrain	Forest tracks and paths are obvious and clearly marked, but are steep and rugged in places.
Refreshment	Bars in Vilaflor.
Transport	Regular daily buses serve Vilaflor from Playa de Las Américas, Los Cristianos and Granadilla.
Waymarked route(s)	Route uses PR TF 72 and GR 131.

The Camino de Chasna was an important route that actually pre-dated the Conquest. It was restored between Vilaflor and the curious *Paisaje Lunar*, marked as the PR TF 72, and later incorporated into the GR 131. Other restored paths allow a return to Vilaflor.

Start below the church of San Pedro in **Vilaflor**, around 1465m (4805ft). There is a map-board at the bottom of the plaza. Walk down a road and turn left, down and up Calle El Canario. Turn right down another road, then left after a house, as signposted along a stone-paved path. A rugged path drops into the terraced **Barranco del Chorillo**. Cross its bed as flashed red/yellow/white, for both the GR 131 and PR TF 72. Follow a track uphill, then turn right up a narrower walled path, which becomes a track. ▶

Look back to the oldest part of Vilaflor, the buildings clustered around the church, and the water-bottling plant above them.

The track is variously stony, rocky or stone-paved, climbing past pines and tagasaste. A water pipe runs alongside and the path is gentler as it passes a farm at **Galindo**, where there are concrete terraces on the left and almonds on the right. Climb further and turn right at the top. Walk down a narrow path that becomes a broad, stone-paved path down into the **Barranco de las Mesas**. Tajinaste grows in the bed of the

▲ *Roque del Encaje*

'Paisaje Lunar'

Barranco de las Arenas

Barranco Ers del Carnero

El Marrubial

Montaña Colorada

N

0   1 km

Walk 20

to Madre del Agua

to Boca de Tauce

Forestry Road

Galindo

Los Llanitos

Forestry Road

Barranco de las Mesas

Lomo Chabeña

Hotel Alba

Walk 20

SF

VILAFLOR

Barranco del Chorillo

to Arona and Los Cristianos

b a r - ranco, and the path climbs to a forest road.

Turn right and quickly left as sign-posted, climbing up stone steps to continue along the path. A three-way

Curious fluted columns of eroded light-coloured ash at the Paisaje Lunar

signpost is reached, where the PR TF 72 heads left and right, while the GR 131 heads only left. Keep left and the path winds up a rocky stony slope, passing a big pine tree with stone seats alongside. Climbing higher, the path becomes easier and there are glimpses of Guajara towering above the pine forest.

Cross a narrow track and later cross a broad track. Go straight up past a barrier gate up a steep and stony track. This becomes gentler as it passes the ruins of **El Marrubial**. A steep and winding stretch later climbs through beds of crumbling, gravelly light-coloured pumice, or *jable*. The track is gentler again, crossing the bed of the **Barranco Erís del Carnero**, climbing past pines and broom to reach a junction.

Keep right, pass an old water channel and avoid another path climbing to the left. A signpost is reached around 2000m (6560ft), where there is a view back to the prominent **Roque del Encaje**. The GR 131 climbs left, while the PR TF 72 drops right, steeply and ruggedly, to a viewpoint for the nearby *Paisaje Lunar* and its eroded, fluted cream-coloured columns of volcanic ash. Continue down the path, crossing a crumbling water channel and passing pines, tagasaste and rock rose, to reach another viewpoint where a notice-board explains about the formation of the columns. A signpost points back and ahead for Vilaflor, so keep walking ahead.

The path drops, turns round a little barranco and makes a gentle traverse through the forest. When a complex junction is reached, keep walking ahead as signposted. There is a drystone wall to the left along a broad straight stretch of track below **Montaña Colorada**. Another signpost points ahead along a broad path which drops, crosses a track and then crosses the gentle **Barranco Erís del Carnero**.

The path continues over a rise and almost reaches a forest road, but runs roughly parallel. A ruin and a big pine tree are passed at **Los Llanitos**. A steep and gritty descent leads to the forest road then, just around a bend, the path is marked on the right, climbing steeply then dropping to a three-way signpost passed earlier in the

Good signposting and waymarking links paths and tracks on the way back to Vilaflor

day. Turn left and follow the path downhill, going down a few stone steps to land on the forest road again.

The continuation of the PR TF 72 and GR 131 is simply a case of retracing the earlier footsteps of the day, across the **Barranco de las Mesas**, past the farm at **Galindo**, and so back to **Vilaflor**.

WALK 21
Boca de Tauce to Chirche

Start	Boca de Tauce
Finish	Chirche
Distance	15km (9½ miles)
Total Ascent	250m (820ft)
Total Descent	1450m (4760ft)
Time	5hrs
Terrain	Winding paths and tracks, mostly downhill, with some climbing, on steep, forested or scrub-covered slopes.
Refreshment	Bars at Chirche.
Transport	One daily bus serves Boca de Tauce from Playa de las Américas, Los Cristianos and Vilaflor. Occasional buses link Chirche with Guía de Isora.
Waymarked route(s)	Route uses Sendero 18 and PR TF 70.

This walk starts at a high level, just inside the national park. It quickly leaves the park and descends through pine forest, traversing a series of rugged barrancos while gradually losing height. The finish is at Chirche, above Guía de Isora, where a network of walking routes is available.

Boca de Tauce, a rugged gap at 2048m (6719ft), just inside the Parque Nacional del Teide, can be reached by bus every morning. There is a road junction, and a building stands near the Vilaflor road, where the national park trail Sendero 18 starts. Follow this narrow path and undulate gently between a rugged lava flow and a series of dramatic cliffs and pinnacles on the face of **Montaña del Palo**. The path climbs onto the lava flow for a while, then drops onto older light-coloured pumice, passing broom and other scrub. Look out for patches of 'ropy' lava. When a path junction is reached, head left up to a track. Turn left along the track to follow it over a crest, through the gap of **Boca de Chavao**, at 2075m (6808ft).

Lava flows reach the base of jagged outcrops near Boca de Tauce

Watch for a
path descending to the left,
flanked by stones, avoiding a bendy
stretch of the track on a forested slope. The
way is flashed yellow/white as the PR TF 70
and later lands on the track. Turn left to cross the
bed of a barranco, go through a barrier gate and
around bends. Watch for a path flashed yellow/
white on the right, and follow it down through forest, across a dip, up and gently down, before it runs
almost level. Turn right as marked and signposted
at a path intersection, winding downhill to cross two

*The solitary forestry
house passed on
the way to the
Barranco de Tágara*

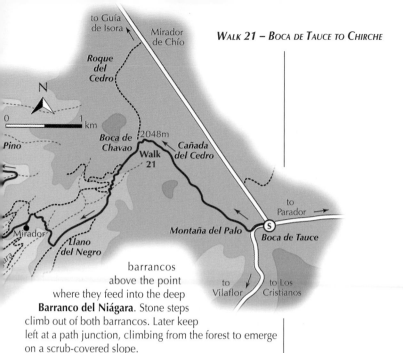

barrancos above the point where they feed into the deep **Barranco del Niágara**. Stone steps climb out of both barrancos. Later keep left at a path junction, climbing from the forest to emerge on a scrub-covered slope.

A short spur path on the left leads to an interesting hilltop **mirador** on Montaña Tafosaya, at 1885m (6184ft). ▶ The other path to the right continues onwards and runs down a scrub-covered slope bearing a few tagasaste bushes. Pass a stump of rock and drop past a little white weather station, crossing a track as signposted among fine light-coloured pumice where there are a few pines. Go down and up past more tagasaste and rampant mixed scrub. Cross a track in a dip and zigzag down into a barranco to cross the lip of a dry waterfall. Make an undulating traverse across a slope of tagasaste back into pine forest. Keep straight ahead to a **forestry house** at a track junction.

Turn right and climb a path running parallel to a concrete water channel. Cross the channel and head downhill, then keep right as marked, steeply uphill with stone steps, to reach a cliff. Turn left to walk along a level path beneath it. There is a slight rise, then go down past stout

Look down to the coast, with views stretching from Roque del Conde to Masca.

109

pines to cross the **Barranco de Tágara**, where the water flows from the Galería Montaña del Cedro o Tágara.

A rising traverse leads up from the barranco bed, then a falling traverse leads out of the barranco completely. Long, sweeping zigzags lead down into the **Barranco Bermejo**, and there is a slight ascent to cross the bed. Leave the forest to traverse across a more scrub-covered slope. At the top, swing right across a ridge and avoid two paths heading to the right. Keep left and wind down a dusty ridge path, passing bushy scrub and at one point a few pines. ◄ Further down the ridge, pass a circular *era*, or threshing floor.

Look back to spot Pico Viejo and El Teide.

Keep winding down the ridge, dropping down a little rock-step later. Drift to the right, and swing left below a rocky slope, then right along the ridge again. The rugged path passes cistus and a few pines, winding down to valley tracks. Walk down a track past vines, then follow a rugged path across a road and down into the village of **Chirche**, around 850m (2790ft). Walk down the road, past the church, and past the Bar Restaurante Brasas de Chirche. Bear in mind that bus services to nearby Guía de Isora are very limited and only run on weekdays. However, it is only a short run by taxi.

Paths wind across forested slopes, in and out of the Barranco de Tágara and Barranco Bermejo

VALLE DE LA OROTAVA

Looking to the snow-capped summit of El Teide from the centre of Puerto de la Cruz

The Valle de la Orotava rises steeply from the city of Puerto de la Cruz, on the north coast of Tenerife, to the northern fringes of the Parque Nacional del Teide. The steep slopes above the city are piled high with cultivation terraces, where the town of La Orotava and several little villages are located. The cultivated slopes give way to laurisilva cloud forest and extensive pine forest, protected as the Parque Natural de Corona Forestal. Many routes have been signposted and waymarked in recent years, particularly in the forests, and these are popular with walkers.

Four walks are offered in this area, and it is possible to switch from one route to another around the popular outdoor recreational area of La Caldera. Walk 22, the Camino de Candelaria, crosses the high crest of Tenerife and was once a major pilgrim route. Walk 25 starts on the edge of the Parque Nacional, and has several links with other routes branching from El Portillo. All the routes in this area also link with the long-distance GR 131 across the high crest of Tenerife.

There is plenty of accommodation available in Puerto de la Cruz, and the Valle de la Orotava is well-served by buses climbing from the city, though only one bus per day goes to and from the Parque Nacional.

WALK 22

Camino de Candelaria – Aguamansa to Arafo

Start	Aguamansa
Finish	Arafo
Distance	13km (8 miles)
Total Ascent	1020m (3345ft)
Total Descent	1545m (5070ft)
Time	5hrs
Terrain	Mostly steep forested slopes with a narrow winding path. The final steep descent is by road.
Refreshment	Bars at Aguamansa and Arafo.
Transport	Regular daily buses serve Aguamansa from Puerto de la Cruz, while Arafo is served daily from Güímar, Candelaria and Santa Cruz.
Waymarked route(s)	Partly signposted as Camino de Candelaria.

In the past pilgrims walked coast-to-coast across Tenerife, from Puerto de la Cruz, up through the Valle de la Orotava, as high as 2000m (6560ft) at La Crucita, and down the other side to Candelaria. The route between Aguamansa and Arafo remains free of tarmac.

Start on a road bend above **Aguamansa**, where there is a map-board and signposts for the PR TF 35 and the Camino de Candelaria. Walk up a stone-paved path that immediately gives way to a rugged path worn to bedrock among pines and heather trees. Turn left up a track, left beside a building, then almost immediately right up a winding path. Cross the track and walk straight up another track, now among laurisilva and pines. Reach another track and a shelter at **Pero Gil**, where there are signs for the Camino de Candelaria.

Cross over the track and climb to the right of the shelter. The path is broad and winds uphill, passing a couple of little wayside shrines. Note the tall, stout eucalyptus among the pines. Cross a track and climb a narrow, well-worn winding path. Cross over another path, which is signposted as the PR TF 35. ◄

Used on Walk 23.

A forest shelter at Pero Gil by the Camino de Candelaria

The Camino de Candelaria is now a narrow winding path worn into a deep groove in crumbling volcanic ash. The pine forest thins out at a higher level and the path winds past a thin wall-like igenous dyke. ▶ The pine cover becomes patchy, with areas of broom, tagasaste and other bushy scrub. The path winds up a crumbling red slope, occasionally rocky, then drifts to the left.

Step over another wall-like dyke and cross a bare, crumbling slope. This gentle traverse is followed by a steep, winding path up a rocky nose. The path again drifts left, past patchy pines and bushy scrub, reaching a road. There are lots of signs, for the Parque Nacional del Teide, Corona Forestal and **La Crucita**, at almost 2000m (6560ft). Cross the road for a very limited view from a mirador. ▶

Pass the barrier gate beside the mirador and walk down a broad ash track into pine forest. The national park Sendero 17 heads up to the right, but continue down the track onto bare ash slopes, watching for another path down to the left. This cuts out a bend from the track, crossing it further downhill on **Lomo del Agua**.

Zigzag carefully down a path worn into loose red ash and pumice, passing a little shrine. Continue down among pines, tagasaste and broom. When views allow, look around to see thick multi-coloured beds of volcanic ash gradually crumbling away. The path lands on the track again, so turn right to follow it a short way. When

Views stretch from the top of El Teide, down through the forest and the Valle de la Orotava, to Puerto de la Cruz.

Arafo is just visible, with Gran Canaria across the sea.

113

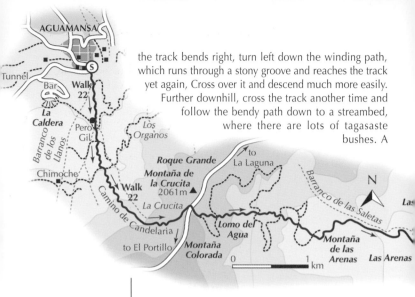

the track bends right, turn left down the winding path, which runs through a stony groove and reaches the track yet again, Cross over it and descend much more easily. Further downhill, cross the track another time and follow the bendy path down to a streambed, where there are lots of tagasaste bushes. A

Looking down through the Valle de la Orotava from a break in the forest

bouldery stretch of path runs down beside the streambed, then a gentle path leads onwards through dense pine forest.

Come out of the forest to face the big black ash dome of **Montaña de las Arenas**, and enjoy views around the

valley while crunching along an ash path. ▶ Join the track again, but before it runs back into forest, turn right down another black ash path, with views down to the built-up land near the coast. Join and follow the track straight ahead, across the foot of the black ash cone. The *Finca Privada* notice painted on a barrier gate forbids motorists, not walkers. When the track forks, keep left and keep crunching down the clearest track on the broad, bare black ash slopes. Chestnut trees have been established further down. Turn left past a **stone hut**, then quickly

The volcano is one of three that erupted early in 1705. Another, Volcán de Fasnia, is seen on Walk 26.

left again down another track. Keep left yet again to follow a well-worn stony path through rock rose, back into forest.

A winding stony path descends among pines and heather trees. There are lots of rugged short-cuts, but it is best to stay on the gentlest path throughout. This eventually crosses a concrete water channel and the undergrowth contains rock rose and cistus. The path becomes stonier and eventually follows another water channel across a terrace of chestnut trees. The path winds tightly and is stony, roughly stone-paved or unevenly rocky. It passes cultivated and tangled slopes and lands on a narrow road.

Turn left down the road, which is quite steep, passing farms and houses around **El Pinarete**. Avoid a turning to the right, but later, make a left turn followed by a right turn to stay on the broadest roads. Drop past the Restaurante Añavingo and a water mill built in 1895. The road drops straight through **Arafo**, and Calle La Libertad leads to the church and plaza in the centre. For the bus station, however, turn right just beforehand along Avenida Reyes de España. ▶

Arafo is known as 'Pueblo de la Musica' and has a good range of facilities.

WALK 23

La Caldera and Camino El Topo

Start/Finish	La Caldera
Distance	15km (9½ miles)
Total Ascent/Descent	600m (1970ft)
Time	5hrs
Terrain	Mostly forested paths, often steep and rugged, and sometimes on exposed cliffs.
Refreshment	Bar at La Caldera.
Transport	Regular daily buses serve La Caldera from Puerto de la Cruz.
Waymarked route(s)	Route includes PR TF 35 and GR 131.

La Caldera is a popular recreational area on forested slopes high above Puerto de la Cruz. A convoluted waymarked trail climbs across forested and rocky slopes, and is sometimes very steep and exposed. Contained within this route is the short circular 'Ruta del Agua', or Walk 24.

Start at the bus stop at **La Caldera**, at almost 1200m (2935ft). The car park is on a gentle slope, so head for the slightly higher end where there is a big sign for Chimoche and a signpost for the PR TF 35. Go down steps and follow a path in dense forest. It is important to turn right, even though the path is marked with an 'X'. Go down the winding path and cross the access road for La Caldera, as flashed yellow/white. Continue down the path and turn sharp left to zigzag down a broader path to the road just above **Aguamansa**, where there is a bus shelter and a notice explaining walking routes.

Look at the notice; a track climbs left from it, and a path is signposted immediately left again, as the PR TF 35. Avoid the nearby road and quickly reach another notice and signposts, including the stone-paved Camino de Candelaria (Walk 22). Just downhill a bit, round a road bend, is the PR TF 35. Go down flights of stone steps and

A narrow stretch of path has been cut around the Barranco de la Madre

down through a rock-walled barranco to reach a road bend and signpost. Keep right and follow the road, Camino de Mamio, over a rise and down through another barranco, almost to 1000m (3280ft). Turn right uphill at a junction along the Camino Nuevo. The road climbs past cultivated plots and chestnuts, becoming a path.

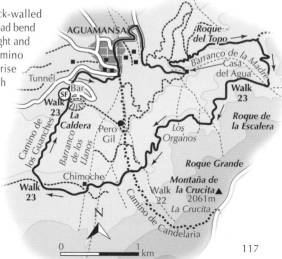

117

Fencing, handrails and cables are provided on some of the exposed cliff paths

The path climbs into a forest of laurisilva and pines, with a rock wall to the left, and crosses the bed of the barranco. Stone steps and zigzags appear as the path climbs steeper. Reach a track and signposts at a stone-built house, **Casa del Agua**, around 1150m (3775ft). ▸ Turn left as signposted for the Camino El Topo, which is also the course of the GR 131, Walk 45. Cross a stone bridge over the **Barranco de la Madre**, rise gently and fork right at a track junction.

The Ruta del Agua, Walk 24, climbs up steps from the building.

Turn right up stone steps as signposted and climb the forested slope towards **Roque del Topo**. Cross a track and continue winding uphill, past a curved stone seat. Level out a couple of times on the forested crest and zigzag steeply up to a rocky outcrop and a signposted path junction, around 1550m (5085ft). Turn right and make a gently undulating traverse, then go down a broad, sweeping zigzag and along another traverse with steep ups and downs. There is a view down the valley, while the vegetation is quite mixed and includes tagasaste trees. A cable is provided for turning a rocky corner, then cross the rocky **Barranco de la Madre**, using a very convoluted path in and out of it.

The path is rather narrow as it clings to a rocky slope, rising and making a quick zigzag. It continues more gently and undulating, then zigzags down from bushy scrub into pines. It runs out into a sheer-walled gully and crosses the bed of a barranco, beneath a looming pinnacle of rock. The narrow path wriggles onwards through forest, and is fenced as it crosses a cliff. Climb among forest and make a sudden left turn, rising and falling, mostly on a well-forested slope. However, turn left down a rocky corner with an open view. Pick a way across a rocky slope below **Los Organos**, with a short cable for safety at one point. Zigzag down the forested slope, then make a lengthy traverse across a rocky slope. A rising traverse across a forested slope intersects with the **Camino de Candelaria**. ▸

Walk 22, which offers a steep and rapid descent.

Keep straight ahead and keep rising, and the path is now broad and cut into a slope of volcanic ash. It later runs down to a signpost in a dip, where a forest track runs gently down to a nearby junction and shelter at

Chimoche. There are eucalyptus trees among the pines, as well as bushy rock rose.

The yellow/white flashed route turns left up a path among the rock rose, climbing past pines onto a slope of pines and heather, to almost 1500m (4920ft). Head down to a track, where there are signposts. Cross the track and go down the **Camino de los Guanches** – a rugged, stony or rocky, tightly-winding path down through the forest. Keep straight ahead downhill at any junctions and cross a water pipeline halfway down. The path becomes easier and even-surfaced, as well as broader. Cross a road as signposted and marked, and return to the car park and nearby bar at **La Caldera**.

WALK 24
La Caldera and Ruta del Agua

Start/Finish	La Caldera
Distance	8km (5 miles)
Total Descent	200m (655ft)
Time	2hrs 30mins
Terrain	Easy forest tracks there and back with a steep ascent and descent on narrow forest paths.
Refreshment	Bar at La Caldera.
Transport	Regular daily buses serve La Caldera from Puerto de la Cruz.
Waymarked route(s)	Route uses GR 131 and PR TF 35.2.

This short route lies entirely within Walk 23, and the two could be covered at the same time. However, the Ruta del Agua stands on its own merit, exploring laurisilva forest, and it can be approached easily from La Caldera. As its name suggests, the area is important for gathering water.

Start at **La Caldera** and walk past the bar until a dirt road heads off to the left. A stout marker indicates the GR 131 and notes that it is also part of the trans-European E7. The broad dirt road is gentle and easy, passing pines, heather trees and bushy rock rose. Cross a bridge over a rocky forested barranco and reach a shelter at **Pero Gil**, where signposts indicate all sorts of routes. Keep following the dirt road and swing easily around another forested barranco. Rise slightly, then head generally downhill. Note how the trees are hung with long, straggly lichen because of the moisture in the air. There is another slight rise and descent, and stone steps are seen climbing on the right. Follow the dirt road to a stone-built house, **Casa del Agua**, around 1150m (3775ft). ▸

The GR 131 stays on the track, and Walk 23 also follows the track here.

The Ruta del Agua climbs up stone steps beside the Casa del Agua

The crumbling arch of an old aqueduct spans a bouldery barranco

The air is often moist, and if it is misty expect the trees to drip water.

Turn right up steps as signposted for the Ruta del Agua. The path leads deceptively easily into the forested **Barranco de la Madre**, then climbs long and steep flights of log steps. Note a stone-built water channel, though this is sometimes buried. Avoid turnings to the left, though at a higher level once the path starts zigzagging, it is worth taking a left turn to see a dry waterfall in the bed of the barranco. The zigzags climb higher, then give way to a level path, around 1300m (4265ft), followed by a gentle traverse down across a steep slope. There are pines and heather trees, with branches dangling skeins of lichen. ◄ There may be glimpses of the Valle de la Orotava and Puerto de la Cruz.

Turn round a rocky corner where there is a fence, and go down winding log steps to cross the bed of another barranco. Climb a bit to pick up and follow another stone-built water channel across the forested slope. The channel soon drops steeply and the path winds steeply down stone and log steps. Cross the channel and make another traverse, crossing the bed of another barranco. Look up it to see the crumbling arch of an aqueduct, and look down to see Puerto de la Cruz. The path rises a bit, then drops, becoming steep as it winds down through dense laurisilva, sometimes with steps. A final short flight of stout stone steps lands on a track at a signpost. This is the same track that was used earlier, so turn left and follow it back to **La Caldera**.

WALK 25
El Portillo to Realejo Alto

Start	El Portillo
Finish	Realejo Alto
Distance	16km (10 miles)
Total Ascent	100m (330ft)
Total Descent	1800m (5905ft)
Time	5hrs
Terrain	An easy mountain path at first, long forest tracks in the middle and a steep and well-wooded descent at the end.
Refreshment	Bar at El Portillo. Bars at Realejo Alto.
Transport	A daily bus serves El Portillo from Playa de las Américas, Los Cristianos, Vilaflor and Puerto de la Cruz. Regular daily buses serve Realejo Alto from Puerto de la Cruz and La Orotava.
Waymarked route(s)	Route uses Sendero 1 and PR TF 40.

Apart from some gentle rising and falling at the start, on the edge of the Parque Nacional, this route is downhill almost all the way. Clear tracks drop through the Parque Natural Corona Forestal, linking with the PR TF 40, which drops steeply to Realejo Alto.

Map continues on page 127

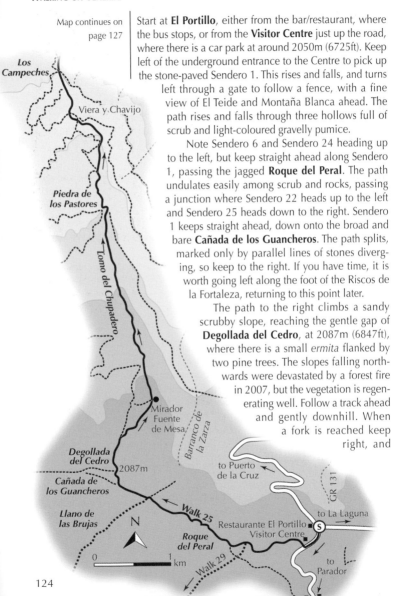

Los Campeches

Viera y Chavijo

Piedra de los Pastores

Lomo del Chupadero

Mirador Fuente de Mesa

Barranco de la Zarza

Degollada del Cedro

2087m

Cañada de los Guancheros

Llano de las Brujas

to Puerto de la Cruz

GR 131

Walk 25

to La Laguna

Restaurante El Portillo
Visitor Centre

N

0   1
         km

Roque del Peral

Walk 29

to Parador

Start at **El Portillo**, either from the bar/restaurant, where the bus stops, or from the **Visitor Centre** just up the road, where there is a car park at around 2050m (6725ft). Keep left of the underground entrance to the Centre to pick up the stone-paved Sendero 1. This rises and falls, and turns left through a gate to follow a fence, with a fine view of El Teide and Montaña Blanca ahead. The path rises and falls through three hollows full of scrub and light-coloured gravelly pumice.

Note Sendero 6 and Sendero 24 heading up to the left, but keep straight ahead along Sendero 1, passing the jagged **Roque del Peral**. The path undulates easily among scrub and rocks, passing a junction where Sendero 22 heads up to the left and Sendero 25 heads down to the right. Sendero 1 keeps straight ahead, down onto the broad and bare **Cañada de los Guancheros**. The path splits, marked only by parallel lines of stones diverging, so keep to the right. If you have time, it is worth going left along the foot of the Riscos de la Fortaleza, returning to this point later.

The path to the right climbs a sandy scrubby slope, reaching the gentle gap of **Degollada del Cedro**, at 2087m (6847ft), where there is a small *ermita* flanked by two pine trees. The slopes falling northwards were devastated by a forest fire in 2007, but the vegetation is regenerating well. Follow a track ahead and gently downhill. When a fork is reached keep right, and

124

then at a pronounced bend turn right to reach a rocky edge at **Mirador Fuente de Mesa**, for a fine view of the Valle de la Orotava.

Walk round the bend on the track and turn right at a junction. The idea is to stay close to the forested edge all the way downhill. The track enters tall pine forest, burnt but regenerating. Further downhill there is a little whitewashed wayside shrine on the left, while tagasaste trees flank the track. A shelter is reached at a complex track junction at **Piedra de los Pastores**, around 1600m (5250ft). Avoid a track doubling back on the right here, but keep ahead down a track signposted for Campeches. Also, avoid a path on the right signposted for Chanajiga.

Keep following the winding track downhill, where laurisilva forest is regenerating. At intersections with other tracks, turn right, except where there is a shelter hut at **Viera y Chavijo**. The track reaches another complex junction at **Los Campeches**, where a track doubling back to the right should be avoided. Instead, take the track signposted 'Icod El Alto', then soon afterwards turn right for 'Pista General Icod El Alto'. There is a short cut down to the left, Vereda de los Junquillos, which could be followed, but

El Teide is prominently in view while walking from El Portillo to Degollada del Cedro

125

Looking down to Realejo Alto and the suburbs of Puerto de la Cruz on the final steep descent

to Icod de los Vinos

REALEJO ALTO

to Puerto de la Cruz

Barranco de la Calera

La Tarasca

Mirador El Asomadero

Barranco Garabato

Walk 25

Los Campeches

the winding track has the benefit of occasional views. ▶

A junction is reached where left is for 'Pista General Icod El Alto', which offers a reasonably easy finish. However, keep right and follow a concrete track flashed yellow/white for the PR TF 40. This leads to a fine viewpoint, the **Mirador El Asomadero**, around 1100m (3610ft). On a clear day it is possible to see all the way from the peak of El Teide to the sea at Puerto de la Cruz. ▶

Leave the viewpoint by walking down chunky stone steps and log steps. Endless tight and steep zigzags drop down through laurisilva, later passing leaning chestnut trees. A couple of caves can be seen, cut into a rock face, while the path later passes along the foot of a big cliff. Heather trees finally give way to a stack of small cultivated plots on a steep slope. Turn right at the bottom, gently uphill beside thickets of cane, to reach a concrete farm track.

Follow the concrete track down through the **Barranco de la Calera**, and always keep to the right-hand side of the bouldery bed of the barranco. Pass sheds and barking dogs, and the track later rises between houses, becoming the Calle el Medio de Arriba. When it reaches a junction with Calle Toscas de Romero, turn left downhill. Turn right at the bottom to reach a couple of bars and a bus stop, or keep walking downhill to see more of **Realejo Alto** (full range of services).

Note the eucalyptus trees towering above the laurisilva.

A tall mast nearby is an unmistakable local landmark.

PARQUE NACIONAL

The amazingly rugged Parque Nacional del Teide boasts a wide range of waymarked trails

Some of the most fascinating walking routes on Tenerife are found high in the centre of the island, in the rocky and barren Parque Nacional del Teide. The immense volcanic cone of El Teide is covered in lava flows that extend onto level gravelly plains, called *cañadas* on Tenerife. A rugged rim of mountains extends in a semicircle, facing back towards El Teide. A splendid network of walking routes, or *senderos*, have been marked and number-coded for many years, and some of these are immensely popular, interesting and incredibly scenic.

Eleven walks are offered in the national park, while those on El Teide are described under a separate heading. Some of the routes are splendid in their own right, while others can be linked together to create longer routes. The long-distance GR 131 also makes its way through the national park. Walkers who wish to base themselves in the national park have only one expensive accommodation option: the Parador Hotel. There is no campsite and wild camping is not permitted. There are bus services from distant resorts and villages, including Puerto de la Cruz, La Orotava, Los Cristianos, Playa de las Américas, Arona and Vilaflor. However, these reach the national park mid-morning and depart mid-afternoon, allowing walkers only a few precious hours of exploration. Using a car for transport allows much longer visits.

There are two interesting visitor centres, one at El Portillo, tel. 922-356000, and the other beside the Parador, tel. 922-373391. They are both dedicated to the geology and natural history of the national park, and both offer plenty of information about walking opportunities.

WALK 26

Izaña and Volcán de Fasnia

Start/Finish	Mirador del Corral del Niño
Distance	8km (5 miles)
Total Ascent/Descent	200m (655ft)
Time	2hrs 30mins
Terrain	Easy tracks and paths on gentle slopes.
Refreshment	None
Transport	None closer than El Portillo, 5km (3 miles) away.
Waymarked route(s)	Route uses Sendero 20.

The white observatories on top of Izaña present a surreal sight and they often stand above a 'sea of clouds'. The rounded red ash slopes nearby are threaded with a network of easy tracks and paths, allowing a close approach to the bare black Volcán de Fasnia.

Start high on the road between El Portillo and Izaña, around 2300m (7545ft), at the **Mirador del Corral del Niño**. Enjoy views of El Teide, then follow the road down to a junction on a gap, signposted for Izaña. Don't go up

A level fenced track passes the Volcán de Fasnia, which erupted in 1705

The volcano erupted in January 1705 – one of three that erupted in Tenerife at that time. Another, Montaña de las Arenas, is seen on Walk 22. ◄

the road to the observatories on the mountain-top, but walk down the broad track marked as Sendero 20. The track bends as it works its way past **Llano el Río**, then levels out below 2200m (7220ft). It is flanked by wooden barriers as it passes the bare black slopes of **Volcán de Fasnia**. ◄

The track rises gently though a gap in the bare black ash; then, when it descends gently, turn right through a barrier gate. Sendero 20 follows a black ash track uphill, back onto scrub-covered slopes, and keeps climbing. It drops slightly into a hollow at **Llano del Chupadero** and forks, so keep right. As the track peters out, a path runs parallel on the left, then on the right. Only a narrow path crosses a red ash gap, over 2310m (7580ft), between the rounded **Montaña de Abreu** and **Montaña de las Vacas**.

Follow the clearest path onwards, meandering past clumps of broom and bare patches, climbing gently as if aiming for another gap between rounded hills. In fact, the path swings right and traverses the slopes of **Montaña de**

One of the observatories at Izaña on a chilly winter morning

la Carniceria. Simply stay on the broad red ash path, with a view of El Teide behind, possibly Gran Canaria far across the 'sea of clouds', with the observatories on Izaña appearing later. The path suddenly joins a road at a car park at **Corral del Niño**, and a right turn leads quickly back to the mirador where the walk started.

WALK 27
El Portillo and Alto de Guamasa

Start/Finish	El Portillo
Distance	4km (2½ miles)
Total Ascent/Descent	100m (330ft)
Time	1hr 15mins
Terrain	Easy paths on rugged slopes.
Refreshment	Bar at El Portillo.
Transport	Daily buses serve El Portillo from Puerto de la Cruz, Vilaflor, Los Cristianos and Playa de las Américas.
Waymarked route(s)	Route uses Sendero 14.

Walkers using buses to reach the national park may find themselves at El Portillo in the afternoon, with time to spare before the bus leaves. There is a bar restaurant and a nearby Visitor Centre, but there is also a short circular walk available over Alto de Guamasa.

The GR 131, or Walk 44, heads left downhill.

Leave the bar/restaurant at **El Portillo**, around 2040m (6695ft), and cross the triangular road junction opposite. Turn left to take Sendero 14 as marked, keeping right uphill at a junction. ◀ The path winds and climbs gently up a scrub-covered slope, then there is a definite left turn along a rising traverse on slopes of pumice. Views embrace El Teide, beyond El Portillo, with Guajara and Topo de la Grieta also prominent. Forested slopes fall to the Valle de la Orotava and Puerto de la Cruz. Look along a high crest to catch a glimpse of Anaga beyond.

The path loses views as it wanders into a crater on **Alto de Guamasa**. Climb out of this to see the observatories on top of Izaña. The path almost touches 2100m (6890ft) before heading gently downhill. Keep right at a junction, and the next right turn leads to a circular arrangement of stone seats on a gap. Keep left instead to follow a gently rising track to a car park. Turn right and walk down the road, through a cutting, to return to **El Portillo**.

The Restaurante El Portillo, at the start of the walk, with El Teide rising far beyond

WALK 28

El Portillo and Arenas Negras

Start/Finish	El Portillo
Distance	8km (5 miles)
Total Ascent/Descent	350m (1150ft)
Time	2hrs 30mins
Terrain	Easy tracks and paths on gentle slopes.
Refreshment	Bar at El Portillo.
Transport	Daily buses serve El Portillo from Puerto de la Cruz, Vilaflor, Los Cristianos and Playa de las Américas.
Waymarked route(s)	Route uses Senderos 2 and 4.

This is a simple circuit from El Portillo, using clear paths and tracks. It wanders between the rounded Montaña El Cerrillar and Montaña Punta de Maja, then crunches down slopes of black volcanic ash on Montaña de las Arenas Negras, following an easy track back to El Portillo.

Start at **El Portillo**, either from the bar/restaurant, where the bus stops, or from the **Visitor Centre** just up the road, where there is a car park, around 2050m (6725ft). Cross the road from the Visitor Centre, pass a barrier gate and follow a clear track across a dip full of bare, gravelly pumice. The track climbs to a fork, where Sendero 4 is to the right and Sendero 2 is to the left. Turn left and climb up a slope of broom and other scrub. When the track bends right there is a chain across it, so keep left up a well-trodden path instead.

There are fine views over the eastern part of the national park, dominated of course by El Teide. However, the view changes and becomes less dramatic as height is gained on the flanks of **Montaña El Cerrillar**. There is a slight descent, then the track makes a sweeping zigzag right and left, gaining a view of the solar observatories on top of Izaña. The path crunches through a broad and

gentle gap beside **Montaña Punta de Maja**, touching 2300m (7545ft). ▶

El Teide and Guajara appear in view ahead.

Alto de Guamasa, seen on the climb from El Portillo, around the slopes of Montaña El Cerrillar

The path runs very gently down through an area strewn with honeycombed rocks, with the plain of **Llano de Maja** to the left. The path swings round to the right and runs close to the edge of a barranco cut into soft multi-coloured beds of volcanic ash, capped by a protective lava flow. Crunch down the bare black ash slopes, and the path zigzags down past **Montaña de las Arenas Negras**. There is plenty of scrub further downhill, but the path also wanders down a gentle slope of ill-sorted stones, gravel, grit, sand and dust, all washed down through the barranco.

Join a track, which is Sendero 4, and turn right to follow it on the level for a while. It climbs a little across a bare stony slope, then descends gently through a sort of valley full of scrub. Pass a barrier gate and follow the stretch of the track that was used earlier in the day, across the dip full of bare gravelly pumice. Pass a barrier gate and cross the road to reach the **Visitor Centre**, or turn right down the road to return to **El Portillo**.

The path descends from Montaña de las Arenas Negras into a dry and dusty barranco

The path winds gently down gravelly slopes with a fine view of El Teide

WALK 29
El Portillo and Montaña Blanca

Start/Finish	El Portillo
Alternative Finish	Montaña Blanca car park
Distance	22km (13½ miles)
Total Ascent/Descent	750m (2460ft)
Time	7hrs
Terrain	Mostly gently-graded gravel paths, becoming steep and soft, linking with a track onto the mountain.
Refreshment	Bar at El Portillo.
Transport	Daily buses serve El Portillo and the Montaña Blanca car park from Puerto de la Cruz, Vilaflor, Los Cristianos and Playa de las Américas.
Waymarked route(s)	Route uses Senderos 1, 6, 7 and 22.

A huge desert-like area between El Portillo and El Teide is covered by light-coloured, lightweight gravelly pumice, or *jable*. A network of paths runs through it, offering routes to and from Montaña Blanca. It is also possible to continue onto El Teide with reference to Walk 37.

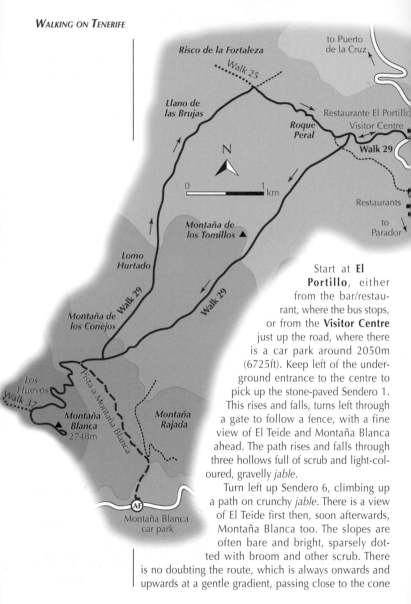

to Puerto
de la Cruz

Risco de la Fortaleza

Walk 25

*Llano de
las Brujas*

Restaurante El Portillo
Visitor Centre

*Roque
Peral*

Walk 29

N

0   1
km

Restaurants

*Montaña de
los Tomillos* ▲

to
Parador

*Lomo
Hurtado*

Walk 29

Walk 29

*Montaña de
los Conejos*

*Los
Huevos*
Walk 37

Pista a Montaña Blanca

*Montaña
Blanca*
2748m ▲

*Montaña
Rajada*

AF

Montaña Blanca
car park

Start at **El
Portillo**, either
from the bar/restau-
rant, where the bus stops,
or from the **Visitor Centre**
just up the road, where there
is a car park around 2050m
(6725ft). Keep left of the underground entrance to the centre to
pick up the stone-paved Sendero 1.
This rises and falls, turns left through
a gate to follow a fence, with a fine
view of El Teide and Montaña Blanca
ahead. The path rises and falls through
three hollows full of scrub and light-coloured, gravelly *jable*.

Turn left up Sendero 6, climbing up
a path on crunchy *jable*. There is a view
of El Teide first then, soon afterwards,
Montaña Blanca too. The slopes are
often bare and bright, sparsely dotted with broom and other scrub. There
is no doubting the route, which is always onwards and
upwards at a gentle gradient, passing close to the cone

of **Montaña de los Tomillos**. Later, the slope is bare and steep, and as the path climbs, it passes a cairn at a junction where Sendero 22 heads down to the right. ▶ Keep climbing to reach a track and a large sign, at almost 2550m (8365ft).

The dusty white track is designated as Sendero 7 and is followed by turning right and climbing round several bends. During the ascent many huge, round dark boulders are passed. These are *Los Huevos del Teide*, or 'Eggs of Teide', lumps of lava that have become detached from the lava flows seen higher up the mountain, and have rolled down the slopes to where they now rest. When a junction is reached, El Teide rises directly ahead, while a left turn leads gently onto **Montaña Blanca**; to a shoulder rather than a summit. The track ends with a short circular loop near the 2748m (9016ft) top ▶

Retrace your steps down the winding track to return to the large sign and head back down the path. When a junction and cairn are reached, turn left to follow Sendero 22, which is a less obvious path, passing left of two large boulders. Keep walking down from **Montaña de los Conejos**, either on gravelly pumice, or weaving between jagged outcrops of lava. The path is drawn into

Using the path immediately, without climbing Montaña Blanca, saves 6.5km (4 miles) there and back, and 200m (655ft) of ascent and descent.

Walk 37 can be used to climb to the summit of El Teide.

Looking back towards El Teide while following the path back down to El Portillo

a little valley and passes more broom on gentle stony slopes. Keep straight ahead where another path heads left. The path seems to be heading for the cliffs of Risco de la Fortaleza, but swings right up a rocky slope. Meander gently and easily through scrub, reaching a junction and noticeboard.

Turn right to follow Sendero 1, which is broad and undulating, with views of El Teide. Keep straight ahead at junctions where Sendero 24 and Sendero 6 climb to the right. The final stretch is simply a matter of retracing the earliest steps of the day to return to the Visitor Centre at **El Portillo**.

WALK 30
El Filo to Parador

Start	Km39 on the road east of El Portillo
Finish	Parador
Distance	21km (13 miles)
Total Ascent	475m (1560ft)
Total Descent	575m (1885ft)
Time	9hrs
Terrain	A good track most of the way, with gentle gradients. A short climb, followed by a longer rugged descent, then easy to the finish.
Refreshment	Cafeteria los Roques at the Parador.
Transport	Daily buses serve El Portillo, 4km (2½ miles) from the start, and the Parador, from Puerto de la Cruz, Vilaflor, Los Cristianos and Playa de las Américas.
Waymarked route(s)	Route includes Senderos 8, 5 and 4.

This route starts easily and follows an easy high-level track mostly above 2300m (7545ft). There are views of El Teide, Guajara and other peaks around Las Cañadas. Leaving the track, a rugged path crosses Montaña de Pasajiron, before a rocky descent from the mountains.

The starting point is 4km (2½ miles) up the road from El Portillo, in the direction of La Esperanza. A track heads off to the right at the **Km39 sign**, around 2250m (7380ft), and there is a notice at a barrier gate for Sendero 8. The route is described as *El Filo – Along the Crest of the Circo Cañadas*. El Teide is in view and remains in view most of the day.

The gently undulating track presents no problems and is easy to follow. It has a long wooden barrier on the right as it passes the broad stony plain of **Llano de Maja**. A gentle climb leads to a broad gap between two rounded hills at **Degollada de Abreu**, at 2315m (7595ft). There is a little cross on the gap and the track swings right across a gentle broom-covered slope, with Gauajara far ahead and Gran Canaria seen far to the left, floating on a 'sea of clouds'.

to El Portillo ← S Km39
Mirador del Corral del Niño
Walk 30
to La Laguna

Montaña de Carniceria
2379m ▲

Montaña Punta de Maja ▲
Montaña de Enmedia ▲
2362m

Llano de Maja

Montaña de Abreu
▲ 2406m

2315m
Degollada de Abreu

Montaña Vista de los Infantes ▲

Map continues on page 142

The view from Llano de los Infantes embraces El Teide and Guajara on either side of Las Cañadas

141

This appears quite innocuous from this side, but looks impressively rugged from below on Walk 43.

Stay on the main track, avoiding lesser ones. When a broad gap is approached near **Llano de los Infantes**, watch out for a notice-board on the right. There is a splendid view of El Teide and Guajara, with the lava-filled *cañadas* between them. The view is lost as the track climbs across the slopes of **Risco Verde**. ◄ Views reappear on the way down to another gap and a track junction. Left leads down into pine forests, so keep straight ahead, even though it is marked *sin salida*, meaning no exit.

Views are lost as the track rises on **Mesa del Obispo**, but are restored as it crosses a dip, though Guajara will not be seen for some time. Climb across the slopes of

Map continues on page 145

Montaña Vista de los Infantes ▲

Cañada de Diego Hernández

Walk 43 – GR 131

to El Portillo →

Llano de los Infantes

Risco Verde ▲

N

0   1 km

Cañada de las Pilas

El Pasero

Cañada de la Angostura

Walk 30

Mesa del Obispo

Montaña de la Angostura ▲

Cañada de la Grieta

Topo de la Grieta ▲

Valle Blanco

Montaña de la Angostura and note lots of tajinaste

growing. Looking ahead jagged peaks can be seen, and a crumbling black gap is reached where there is a fine view of El Teide. A short steep climb up a stone-buttressed track leads onwards round a mountainside, then down to a crumbling gap of white gravelly pumice, or *jable*.

The prominent peak of Topo de la Grieta faces El Teide across Las Cañadas

The prominent peak of **Topo de la Grieta** faces El Teide, then the track descends very gently across the white crumbling slopes of **Valle Blanco**. A rising traverse looks down on extensive pine forest, which may be covered in clouds. There is a sudden pronounced right turn, followed by a left turn, as the rough and stony track climbs and then runs gently across the mountainside.

Watch for a path slicing up to the right, marked as Sendero 8. This is narrow, dusty and stony, but clear and obvious across the slopes of **Roque de la Grieta**. It makes a traverse to a crumbling gap at 2413m (7917ft), while below the track runs out of sight and soon expires. ▶ The path winds uphill and finds an easy breach through a

There is a great view from the gap, with Guajara and El Teide facing each other across the rugged *cañadas*.

143

cliff, running level and narrowly missing the 2529m (8297ft) summit of **Montaña de Pasajiron**.

The path downhill is a winding, crumbling

Looking across Las Cañadas to El Teide before climbing Montaña de Pasajiron

stony affair, with a couple of marker arrows and fine views down to the *cañadas*. However, looking back uphill, the slope

seems remarkably rocky without a trace of a path! When a gap is reached at 2373m (7785ft) on **Degollada de Guajara**, climb up the other side as if heading for Guajara. A large notice-board is reached at a path junction. Use Sendero 15, straight ahead, if you wish to climb Guajara at this point; otherwise turn right down Sendero 5. This is plain and obvious once located. Although stony and narrow, on a rocky scrubby slope, it is fairly easy and leads unerringly down to a notice-board beside a clear track near the broad **Cañada del Montón de Trigo**, around 2200m (7220ft).

Turn left to follow the track over a rise. ▶ Sendero 16 heads right, but keep straight ahead and follow the track downhill, later wriggling around pinnacles and buttresses while rising and falling. A rugged path offers a short-cut through one pronounced bend. A curiously eroded mass of yellow rock at the foot of Guajara is appropriately named **Piedras Amarillas**. Pass a stone cabin and watch for a path on the right, Sendero 4, which leads directly to the **Parador**.

Tall tajinaste is prominent on the rocky slopes, flourishing since grazing was banned in the national park.

WALK 31

Parador and ascent of Guajara

Distance	10km (6¼ miles)
Start/Finish	Parador
Total Ascent/Descent	600m (1970ft)
Time	4hrs
Terrain	A steep, rugged and rocky ascent, with a danger of rock-fall, followed by a rugged descent, but easier paths on the lower parts.
Refreshment	Cafeteria los Roques at the Parador.
Transport	Daily buses serve the Parador from Playa de Las Américas, Los Cristianos, Vilaflor and Puerto de la Cruz.
Waymarked route(s)	Route includes Senderos 4, 31, 15 and 5.

Guajara is the third highest mountain on Tenerife, with only neighbouring El Teide and Pico Viejo standing higher. This route to the top is very steep and rocky in places, with a danger of rock-fall on part of the ascent. A route around the mountain, omitting the summit, is described in Walk 32.

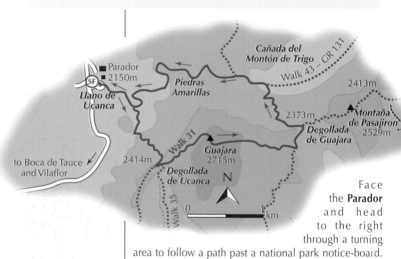

Face the **Parador** and head to the right through a turning area to follow a path past a national park notice-board. The stony path is Sendero 4, running down a gentle slope covered in broom and other scrub. Cross a track and climb a stony path through scrub, noticing prominent tajinaste and a scattering of pines. This path is Sendero 31, climbing onto a gap next to a hill formed of yellow rock. Walk up a blunt ridge past broom, apparently heading for a wall of rock on the skyline ahead.

Sendero 31 heads for El Sombero and is followed on Walk 36. The Valle de Ucanca, down the other side of the gap, is followed to Vilaflor on Walk 35. **Take care not to confuse Walk numbers in this guide with Sendero numbers.**

When the path reaches the rock wall it is pushed up to the right, later swinging left down onto a gap, **Degollada de Ucanca**, at 2414m (7920ft). Guajara towers above, while El Sombrero rises on the ridge in the opposite direction. The distant island of La Palma can be seen far beyond Llano de Ucanca, followed by Pico Viejo, El Teide and Montaña Blanca. ◄ Continue towards Guajara, climbing and winding, steep and stony, rocky and scrubby.

146

The path is pushed to the left up a rising traverse below huge cliffs. Some parts are trodden dusty and white, and there are black boulders of obsidian lying around. The traverse gives way to a bouldery scramble to the summit of **Guajara**, at 2715m (8907ft). There is a square stone-walled enclosure on top, with views facing Pico Viejo, El Teide and Montaña Blanca. Look across the sea to spot the islands of Gran Canaria, El Hierro, La Gomera and La Palma.

There is a very steep and rocky climb onto Guajara from the Degollada de Ucanca

If attempting this route in reverse, walk roughly northwards down a bouldery slope towards Montaña Blanca, watching carefully for a left turn down the traverse.

To leave the summit use Sendero 15, following a path gently downhill, roughly eastwards. It starts zigzagging and becomes gritty, dusty and white underfoot. Keep left at junctions to continue down stony and rocky slopes, undulating to reach a gap at 2373m (7785ft) on **Degollada de Guajara**. A large notice-board is reached at a path junction. Turn left down Sendero 5, which is plain and obvious once located. Although stony and narrow, on a rocky scrubby slope, it is fairly easy and leads unerringly down to a

Tall tajinaste is prominent on the rocky slopes, flourishing since grazing was banned in the national park.

notice-board beside a clear track near the broad **Cañada del Montón de Trigo**, around 2200m (7220ft).

Turn left to follow the track over a rise. ◄ Sendero 16 heads right, so keep straight ahead and follow the track downhill, later wriggling around pinnacles and buttresses while rising and falling. A rugged path offers a short-cut through one pronounced bend. A curiously eroded mass of yellow rock at the foot of Guajara is appropriately named **Piedras Amarillas**. Pass a stone cabin and watch for a path on the right, Sendero 4, which leads directly back to the **Parador**.

An easy track passes the dramatic Piedras Amarillas on the way back to the Parador

WALK 32
Parador and circuit of Guajara

Start/Finish	Parador
Distance	13km (8 miles)
Total Ascent/Descent	1000m (3280ft)
Time	5hrs
Terrain	A steep and rugged climb is followed by a vague valley path, giving way to clearer paths on barren slopes of ash and rock.
Refreshment	Cafeteria los Roques at the Parador.
Transport	Daily buses serve the Parador from Playa de Las Américas, Los Cristianos, Vilaflor and Puerto de la Cruz.
Waymarked route(s)	Route uses Senderos 4, 5, 31, PR TF 72 and GR 131.

This route climbs across gaps on either side of the rugged mountain of Guajara, without making a summit bid. Instead, the Valle de Ucanca can be explored, a detour to the curious *Paisaje Lunar* could be made, and the barren flanks of the mountain can be walked.

Face the **Parador** and head to the right through a turning area to follow a path past a national park noticeboard. The stony path is Sendero 4, running down a gentle slope covered in broom and other scrub. Cross a track and climb a stony path through scrub, noticing prominent tajinaste and a scattering of pines. This path is Sendero 31, climbing onto a gap next to a hill formed of yellow rock. Walk up a blunt ridge past broom, apparently heading for a wall of rock on the skyline ahead.

When the path reaches the rock wall it is pushed up to the right, later swinging left down onto a gap, **Degollada de Ucanca**, at 2414m (7920ft). Guajara towers above, while El Sombrero rises on the ridge in the opposite direction. The distant island of La Palma can be seen far beyond Llano de Ucanca, followed by Pico Viejo, El Teide and Montaña Blanca. ▶ The route

From this gap Walk 31 climbs Guajara and Walk 36 heads for El Sombero.

crosses the gap to go down a vague path that needs to be spotted on a stony slope bearing broom.

Little cairns mark the path, which seems to drift to the right-hand side of the **Valle de Ucanca**. However, watch for it swinging across to the left-hand side soon afterwards. Pick up and follow a path beside a water pipe, though later the path falls below the level of the pipe. Masses of tajinaste grow among the scrub, while later pine trees begin to increase in number. The **Roque del Encaje** appears to block the valley mouth, while the rocky Guajara rises steeply to the left, in awesome tiered cliffs. Keep an eye on the path, passing a small hut

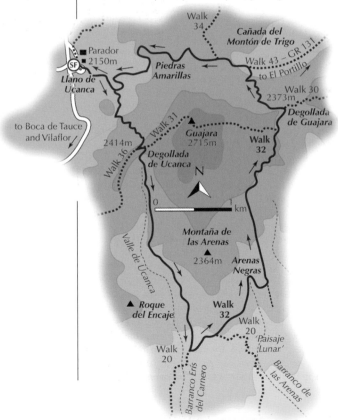

where the water flow is regulated. An old water channel is seen from time to time; the path runs below it for a while, then runs above it. Take care, as this path is vague and overgrown in places. Watch for little cairns and evidence of use, and if a rugged lava flow is reached, drift left to pick up an easier path among the pines. The path becomes clearer, but is soft underfoot as it crosses slopes of ash.

A junction is reached around 1950m (6400ft), with a broad path flanked by parallel lines of stones, flashed red/yellow/white as it is used by both the PR TF 72 and GR 131 trails. Turn left up to a signposted junction where the PR TF 72 drops right, steeply and ruggedly, to a viewpoint for the nearby *Paisaje Lunar*. ▶ The GR 131 climbs left, the path steep and stony among pines, then up slopes of red and black volcanic ash as the pines thin out. Cross the **Barranco de las Arenas**, where creamy boulders stand starkly among black ash.

Climb onto a slope of bare ash where the path is flanked by parallel lines of wooden posts. Hardly anything grows, but there are pines further downhill. Reach a junction where paths are marked by parallel lines of stones, and turn left uphill on soft and crunchy ash. The path appears to head straight for the summit of Guajara,

Walking through snow in the Valle de Ucanca before heading for the Paisaje Lunar

Visited on Walk 20.

151

while Gran Canaria can be seen floating on the 'sea of clouds'. Black ash gives way abruptly to creamy boulders, short of 2400m (7875ft).

The path is trodden to gravel and dust and winds all over the slope, which bears sparse pines and clumps of flowery scrub. Without the path, progress would be dreadfully slow, but it climbs and contours fairly easily, drifting to the right and passing a solitary juniper bush. There is plenty of broom at a higher level and the path reaches a metal post at a junction. ◄ Keep straight ahead, down past crumbling *jable*, a gravelly light-coloured pumice, then the path undulates across a rocky slope to reach a gap, **Degollada de Guajara**, at 2373m (7785ft). Views include Guajara, Pico Viejo, El Teide, Montaña Blanca and nearby Montaña de Pasajiron.

Watch for a path heading downhill, which is plain and obvious once located. Although stony and narrow, on a rocky scrubby slope, it is fairly easy and leads unerringly down to a notice-board beside a clear track near the broad **Cañada del Montón de Trigo**, around 2200m (7220ft). Turn left to follow the track over a

Turning left, the summit of Guajara can be reached using a well-trodden path.

An ash path suddenly gives way to a rocky slope on the way to the Degollada de Guajara

Looking from the Parador to the snow-dusted rocky north face of Guajara

rise. ▶ Sendero 16 heads right, but keep ahead and follow the track downhill, later wriggling around pinnacles and buttresses, while rising and falling. A rugged path offers a short-cut through one pronounced bend. A curiously eroded mass of yellow rock at the foot of Guajara is appropriately named **Piedras Amarillas**. Pass a stone cabin and watch for a path on the right, Sendero 4, which leads directly back to the **Parador**.

Tall tajinaste is prominent on the rocky slopes, flourishing since grazing was banned in the national park.

WALK 33
Parador and Roques de García

Start/Finish	Parador
Distance	4km (2½ miles)
Total Ascent/Descent	150m (490ft)
Time	1hr 30mins
Terrain	Mostly easy and fairly level paths, but occasionally steep and rugged.
Refreshment	Cafeteria los Roques at the Parador.
Transport	Daily buses serve the Parador from Playa de Las Américas, Los Cristianos, Vilaflor and Puerto de la Cruz.
Waymarked route(s)	Route uses Sendero 3.

The Roques de García are incredible, formed of pinnacles and towers, cliffs and buttresses, neatly tied together by an easy and popular path. This area is very busy during the day, so if you are looking for solitude, then make your visit early or late in the day.

The **Parador**, its café and the adjacent Visitor Centre stand at around 2150m (7055ft). Walk away from the hotel, past a chapel, to cross the main road and continue along a road that is virtually a linear car park. The end of the

The Roques de García come in all shapes and sizes and attract crowds of admirers throughout the day

road can get very busy as people mill around viewpoints, climbing up and down stone steps; national park staff strive to keep people on the correct side of roped-off areas as people struggle to take photographs. Depending where people stand, there are splendid views of the adjacent Roques de García, with Pico Viejo, El Teide and other mountains arranged around the level gravel-strewn *cañadas*. There are plenty of interpretative notices to study.

Leave the road-end viewpoint and go down Sendero 3, which starts as an obvious narrow path winding down a steep and stony slope, levelling out around 2030m (6660ft) beside the pyramidal form of **La Catedral**, which is popular with rock-climbers. Pass it, and note a marker for Sendero 26 heading left, but keep straight ahead, now climbing gently, then more steeply. The path goes up a dark, crystalline ropy lava flow that spewed from Pico Viejo during an eruption in 1998. Marvel at nearby pinnacles and narrow clefts, while passing a juniper and pine. Cairns mark the way, which is sometimes across bare rock. Note how the dark lava spilled through a gap and has solidified into a form reminiscent of a waterfall.

The remarkably top-heavy Roque Cinchado, with a snow-dusted El Teide far beyond

Climb between the light-coloured pinnacles of **Torre Blanco**, past a roped edge at the top of the 'lava-fall', at almost 2200m (7220ft). There is a view of the whole southern flank of El Teide as the route heads downhill and levels out. A gentle, winding descent leads easily along the foot of the **Roques de García**, passing one of the most striking pinnacles, the contorted and undercut, top-heavy **Roque Cinchado**. Return to the road and car park, or if catching a bus, to the **Parador**.

WALK 34
Parador and Montaña Majúa

Start/Finish	Parador
Distance	11km (6¾ miles)
Total Ascent/Descent	300m (985ft)
Time	3hrs 30mins
Terrain	A path and tracks gently undulate across gentle, stony and scrub-covered slopes.
Refreshment	Cafeteria los Roques at the Parador.
Transport	Buses serve the Parador from Playa de Las Américas, Los Cristianos, Vilaflor and Puerto de la Cruz.
Waymarked route(s)	Route uses Senderos 19, 16 and 4.

Montaña Majúa is a small hump forever humbled at the foot of the mighty El Teide. An easy path reaches it from the Parador, and good tracks allow a circuit to be made back to the Parador. The whole route is easy, in an area surrounded by much tougher walking routes.

The **Parador**, its café and the adjacent Visitor Centre stand at around 2150m (7055ft). Walk away from the hotel along the access road that runs towards El Teide. Halfway along a notice on the right denotes the start of Sendero 19. The path is level and sandy as it runs past broom and other scrub. Don't worry if it swings right towards Guajara, because when it reaches the foot of

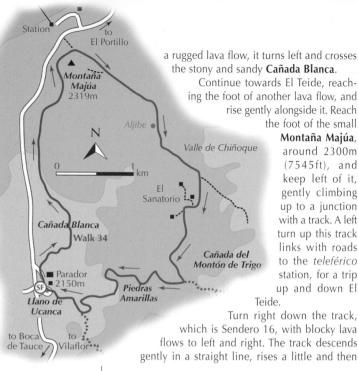

a rugged lava flow, it turns left and crosses the stony and sandy **Cañada Blanca**.

Continue towards El Teide, reaching the foot of another lava flow, and rise gently alongside it. Reach the foot of the small **Montaña Majúa**, around 2300m (7545ft), and keep left of it, gently climbing up to a junction with a track. A left turn up this track links with roads to the *teleférico* station, for a trip up and down El Teide.

Turn right down the track, which is Sendero 16, with blocky lava flows to left and right. The track descends gently in a straight line, rises a little and then

Fairly level areas of stony scrub are crossed between the Parador and the foot of El Teide

descends again. Note a curious half-buried structure to the right, an *aljibe*, which is used for storing water. Avoid turnings to right and left, which may be marked as dangerous due to the presence of bee-hives. After turning a corner the track rises again, and the rugged mountain of Guajara can be seen ahead, except when briefly obscured by masses of jagged lava. ▶ Don't approach the buildings on the right at **El Sanatorio**, a former sanatorium. The track reaches a junction with another prominent track at the foot of Guajara, around 2200m (7220ft).

Turn right to follow the track, which is marked as Sendero 4. It runs downhill, later wriggling around pinnacles and buttresses while rising and falling. A rugged path offers a short-cut through one pronounced bend. A curiously eroded mass of yellow rock at the foot of Guajara is appropriately named **Piedras Amarillas**. Pass a stone cabin and watch for a path on the right, which leads directly back to the **Parador**.

The path to Montaña Majúa passes the jagged snout of an old lava flow

Some sections of the track are quite bendy.

159

Dramatic rock towers are passed as a track is followed back to the Parador

WALK 35

Parador, Valle de Ucanca and Vilaflor

Start	Parador
Finish	Iglesia de San Pedro, Vilaflor
Distance	15km (9½ miles)
Total Ascent	440m (1445ft)
Total Descent	1125m (3690ft)
Time	6hrs
Terrain	Steep and stony paths, vague at times, giving way to clear paths and tracks.
Refreshment	Cafeteria los Roques at the Parador. Bars in Vilaflor.
Transport	Buses serve the Parador from Playa de Las Américas, Los Cristianos, Vilaflor and Puerto de la Cruz. Regular daily buses serve Vilaflor from Playa de Las Américas, Los Cristianos and Granadilla.
Waymarked route(s)	Route includes Sendero 31, PR TF 72 and GR 131.

A rugged path crosses the Degollada de Ucanca, west of Guajara, and can be followed down through the Valle de Ucanca. Bear in mind that it is vague in places, but it eventually links with a clear path. This is waymarked as the PR TF 72 and GR 131, offering routes down to Vilaflor.

Face the **Parador** and head to the right through a turning area to follow a path past a national park notice-board. The stony path is Sendero 4, running down a gentle slope covered in broom and other scrub. Cross a track and climb a stony path through scrub, noticing prominent tajinaste and a scattering of pines. This path is Sendero 31, climbing onto a gap next to a hill formed of yellow rock. Walk up a blunt ridge past broom, apparently heading for a wall of rock on the skyline ahead.

When the path reaches the rock wall it is pushed up to the right, later swinging left down onto a gap, **Degollada de Ucanca**, at 2414m (7920ft). Guajara towers above, while El Sombrero rises on the ridge in the opposite direction. The distant island of La Palma can

Climbing from Las Cañadas towards the Degollada de Ucanca

Two other routes leave this gap, Walk 31 climbing Guajara and Walk 36 heading for El Sombero.

be seen far beyond Llano de Ucanca, followed by Pico Viejo, El Teide and Montaña Blanca. ◄ Continue across the gap to go down a vague path that needs to be spotted on a stony slope bearing broom.

Little cairns mark the path, which seems to drift to the right-hand side of the **Valle de Ucanca**. However, watch for it swinging across to the left-hand side

to El Portillo

Roques de García

Roque Cinchado

■ Parador ■ 2150m

Ⓢ

Piedras Amarillas

La Catedral ▲

Llano de Ucanca

Walk 31

2414m

Guajara ▲ 2715m

to Boca de Tauce and Vilaflor

Walk 36

Degollada de Ucanca

Map continues on page 164

soon afterwards. Pick up and follow a path beside a water pipe, though later the path falls below the level of the pipe. Masses of tajinaste grow among the scrub, while later pine trees begin to increase in number. The Roque del Encaje appears to block the valley mouth, while the rocky Guajara rises steeply to the left, in awesome tiered cliffs. Keep an eye on the path, passing a small hut where the water flow is regulated. An old water channel is seen from time to time. The path runs below it for a while, then runs above it. Take care, as this path is vague and overgrown in places. Watch for little cairns and evidence of use, and if a rugged lava flow is reached, drift left to pick up an easier path among the pines. The path becomes

Walking through snow on the way down through the Valle de Ucanca

clearer, but is soft underfoot as it crosses slopes of ash.

A junction is reached around 1950m (6400ft), with a broad path flanked by parallel lines of stones, flashed red/yellow/white as it is used by both the PR TF 72 and GR 131 trails. Turning right or left offers routes to Vilaflor. ▶

If the left turn is chosen, refer to Walk 20 to the *Paisaje Lunar* and Vilaflor.

Turn right and pass an old water channel, dropping past pines and broom to cross the bed of **Barranco Erís del Carnero**. Climb from this and later wind down steep beds of crumbling gravelly pumice, or *jable*. A gentler stretch of track passes the ruins of **El Marrubial**, then there is a steep and stony descent to a barrier gate. Cross a broad track and later cross a narrow track. A path continues gently downhill, passing a big pine tree with stone seats

If the *Paisaje Lunar* option was taken via Walk 20, turn left here.

alongside. Wind down a rocky stony slope to reach a three-way signpost. ◄ Turn right down stone steps to land on a forest road. Turn quickly left and right as signposted to cross the road.

A path drops into the **Barranco de las Mesas**, where tajinaste grows. A stone-paved path climbs from the barranco, broad, but becoming narrow at the top. Turn left down past a farm at **Galindo**, where there are concrete terraces on the right and almonds on the left, with a water pipe alongside.

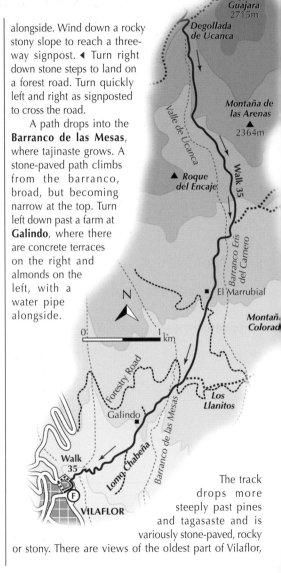

The track drops more steeply past pines and tagasaste and is variously stone-paved, rocky or stony. There are views of the oldest part of Vilaflor,

Following a well-maintained path down through pine forest towards Vilaflor

the buildings clustered around the church, and the water-bottling plant above them.

The track becomes a narrower walled path, winding down to join another track to cross the terraced Barranco del Chorillo. Climb up a stone-paved path as flashed red/yellow/white to reach a house and a road. Turn right up the road, left to go down and up Calle El Canario into **Vilaflor**, then right up another road to reach the plaza and a mapboard, below the church of San Pedro, at around 1465m (4805ft).

WALK 36
Parador to Las Lajas and Vilaflor

Start	Parador
Finish	Iglesia de San Pedro, Vilaflor
Distance	18km (11 miles)
Total Ascent	760m (2495ft)
Total Descent	1445m (4740ft)
Time	7hrs
Terrain	Steep and stony ascent. Mostly easy on top but vague at times, with some scrambling. Mostly clear paths and tracks on the descent through forest.
Refreshment	Cafeteria los Roques at the Parador. Restaurant at Las Lajas. Bars in Vilaflor.
Transport	Daily buses serve the Parador and Las Lajas from Playa de Las Américas, Los Cristianos and Vilaflor. Regular daily buses serve Vilaflor from Playa de Las Américas, Los Cristianos and Granadilla.
Waymarked route(s)	Route uses Senderos 4 and 31.

This route offers one of the easiest walks along the rugged ridge at the south side of the Parque Nacional. Apart from the initial rugged ascent, most of the ridge is broad and gentle. The descent to Las Lajas is stony, and the continuation through forest to Vilaflor is often very stony.

Face the **Parador** and head to the right through a turning area to follow a path past a national park notice-board. The stony path is Sendero 4, running down a gentle slope covered in broom and other scrub. Cross a track and climb a stony path through scrub, noticing prominent tajinaste and a scattering of pines. This path is Sendero 31, climbing onto a gap next to a hill formed of yellow rock. Walk up a blunt ridge past broom, apparently heading for a wall of rock on the skyline ahead.

When the path reaches the rock wall it is pushed up to the right, reaching a point above the gap of **Degollada de Ucanca**, at 2414m (7920ft). Guajara towers beyond the gap and is climbed on Walk 31, but turn right to follow Sendero 31 away from the gap. The distant island of La Palma can be seen far beyond Llano de Ucanca, followed by Pico Viejo, El Teide and Montaña Blanca.

There is a surprisingly easy, narrow, but obvious path with markers and paint blobs. It rises and falls, linking gravelly gaps rather than rocky peaks. From time to time it features excellent views,

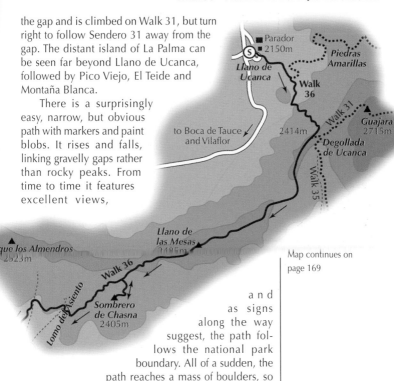

Map continues on page 169

and as signs along the way suggest, the path follows the national park boundary. All of a sudden, the path reaches a mass of boulders, so watch for markers and little cairns, then use your hands to scramble up a rock-face. The path is suddenly easy again, weaving between thickets of broom on the broad crest of **Llano de las Mesas**. ▶

The highest point is difficult to discern, but reaches 2485m (8153ft).

The crest has some bouldery stretches, then narrows to a rocky ridge. A short scramble downwards requires an airy step that some might find unnerving. A gentler path continues along the crest, reaching a junction beside one of the national park boundary signs. Heading left from the sign, a cliff-girt, flat-topped summit is seen, and this is worth a slight detour. A path aims for a rugged breach in the cliffs where a short scramble gains the summit of **Sombrero de Chasna** at 2405m (7890ft).

A view of El Sombrerito, the 'little sombrero', lying north of Las Lajas

If a summit bid isn't required, then follow a marked path downhill from the national park sign, being drawn across a stone-strewn slope into a gentle valley, where pine forest is seen ahead. Keep following the clearest path, which is marked by paint blobs, crossing the valley and later zigzagging down through the forest. There is a slight climb over **Lomo del Asiento** and the path makes an easy crossing of the **Barranco del Cuervo**. The path is clear as it continues descending but, curiously, as it approaches the mountain road it begins to climb again, before dropping to the road beside a ruined building. Follow the bendy road uphill and turn left into the recreational site at **Las Lajas**, around 2100m (6890ft), where there is a small restaurant.

The walk can be ended at Las Lajas, by catching a bus down to Vilaflor and the coast. However, an old trail offers an extension down to Vilaflor, though it is rather rugged in places. Walk to the end of the dirt road through the recreational site, to find a broad turning area. Keep right of this to find a path running downhill, flanked by parallel lines of stones. It becomes a bit vague, but climbs round the slopes of **Montaña de las Lajas**, reaching a rock outcrop and a notice-board. There is a good view northwards to El Sombrero, then the path climbs further and levels out pleasantly.

Heading downhill, note a viewpoint on the right, overlooking Ifonche, otherwise follow the winding, narrow stony path steeply downhill.

Cross the **Barranco del Cuervo** and rise alongside it while peering into its rock-walled depths. Pass a couple more notice-boards while following the dusty path down rather bare and gravelly slopes. Cross a track and continue downhill, then turn left down a track, passing above a **ruin** and crossing a gentle barranco.

The track is very rough and rocky as it climbs, and might be lost if it were not flanked by low stone walls. It eases for a while, passing a notice-board, then becomes rough, stony and rocky while winding downhill, often with water pipes alongside. Pass another notice-board and later reach a junction where another path with a pipe alongside joins, which is part of the GR 131.

Turn left and drop gently towards a covered **reservoir**. Walk down the rugged access track and keep left at a junction, down through forest, levelling out to pass through a cultivated area. Another short stretch through forest leads to a road-end between a football pitch and **Hotel Vill Alba**.

Pass the hotel and keep left at a fork in the road. The Ermita San Roque has a small plaza offering a fine view of Vilaflor. Walk down a stone-paved path and steps beside the road. Cross the main road and follow Calle Los Molinos down into **Vilaflor**, reaching the church of San Pedro and its plaza, around 1465m (4805ft).

A rough and rocky track is followed through pine forest on the way down to Vilaflor

EL TEIDE

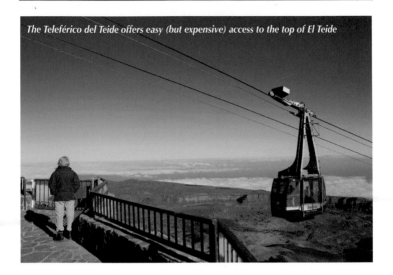

The Teleférico del Teide offers easy (but expensive) access to the top of El Teide

The volcanic peak of El Teide stands in the middle of Tenerife and completely dominates the island. It is the highest mountain on Spanish territory, peaking at 3718m (12,198ft). Many walkers flock to its slopes, but some of them find its steepness off-putting. The mountain is also high enough for some people to be affected by altitude sickness. The 'cure' for this is to descend immediately. The easiest way up the mountain is on the Teleférico del Teide, which takes a mere eight minutes to climb from 2355m to 3555m (7725ft to 11,665ft), but it is of course very popular and weather-dependent. For details and to make advance bookings, tel. 922-010445, www.telefericoteide.com.

Walking routes on El Teide are restricted to only two approaches on the higher slopes, though there are four good starting points available from the roads on the lower slopes. This allows for some variety between ascents and descents. The final summit cone can only be visited by walkers who apply in advance for a permit. To do this, either go in person to an office in Santa Cruz, or apply online; either way, you must produce a passport or identity card, both to apply for the permit and to show on the final ascent along with your permit. There are detailed conditions, rules and regulations that must be followed in order to climb to the summit, so take note of these while applying for a permit or you may be refused access, even at the last minute. Permits are issued for individuals, as well as for groups of up to 10 walkers. It is possible for one person to apply for a permit for a small group of walkers, but read the rules and regulations carefully.

Office – Parque Nacional del Teide, Calle Emilio Calzadilla 5, Planta 4, 38002 Santa Cruz, Tenerife. Tel. 922-922371. Online – www.reservasparquesnacionales.es and click on 'Teide'.

The need for a permit is waived when walkers spend the night at the Refugio Altavista, at 3270m (10,730ft), and continue climbing to the summit in time for sunrise. If this option is taken, it is necessary to leave the summit straight afterwards. It is best to book a bed at the refuge in advance, tel. 922-010440. Give your name and nationality; write down your booking number and quote it on reaching the refuge. Facilities are basic, limited to a heated common room, dormitories with bunk beds, toilets, washbasins, a basic kitchen and a drinks vending machine. Water on the premises must be boiled if used for cooking or drinking. All food supplies must be carried to the refuge and waste must be carried away. Walkers are allowed to stay for one night only, and cannot leave luggage in the building while they climb the mountain. Keep hold of the voucher you are given when you pay to stay in the refuge, as it may need to be produced if anyone asks to see it on the final summit path.

The reward for a successful ascent is an astounding view, embracing the national park, the rest of Tenerife and possibly the other six Canary Islands. Usually, only the summits of the nearest and highest islands are seen above the 'sea of clouds'. Those who reach the summit at sunrise or sunset can marvel as a triangular shadow is thrown across the clouds by El Teide.

Tough and determined walkers who cannot resist a challenge could attempt to climb the 'Three Peaks of Tenerife' by referring to Walk 40.

Care is needed to locate the path climbing from the Roques de Garcia

WALK 37

El Teide via Montaña Blanca

Start/Finish	Montaña Blanca car park
Distance	20km (12½ miles) there and back
Total Ascent/Descent	1400m (4595ft)
Time	9hrs
Terrain	A broad vehicle track climbs gently, then winds more steeply up onto Montaña Blanca. A steep, rugged winding path climbs higher, eventually reaching the summit cone. Note that there is a small risk of altitude sickness, so try to acclimatise first.
Refreshment	None
Transport	Buses serve the Montaña Blanca car park from Playa de Las Américas, Los Cristianos, Vilaflor, El Portillo and Puerto de la Cruz.
Waymarked route(s)	Route uses Senderos 7, 10 and 11.

This is the most popular route to the summit of El Teide. It follows a simple and obvious vehicle track onto the light-coloured pumice slopes of Montaña Blanca, then climbs a steep and rugged path past the Refugio Altavista to reach the top *teleférico* station and the summit.

Either park or arrive by bus at the Montaña Blanca **car park**, around 2350m (7710ft), where there is a huge stone 'map' showing the winding vehicle track used on the first half of the route. Go through a barrier gate and walk up a gravel track, the **Pista a Montaña Blanca**, or Sendero 7. This is bendy and dusty, almost white where vehicles run along it, but flanked by pale yellow slopes of gravelly pumice, or *jable*. Climb and keep left at a junction, continuing gradually up the track, reaching a large sign at almost 2550m (8365ft). ▶

Walk 29 joins here, offering an alternative ascent from El Portillo.

The track keeps climbing, rather more steeply, round several bends. During the ascent many huge, round dark boulders are passed. These are *Los Huevos del Teide*, or 'Eggs of Teide', lumps of lava that have become detached

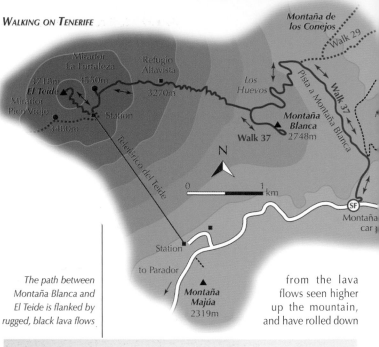

Montaña de
los Conejos

Walk 29

Mirador
La Fortaleza

Refugio
Altavista

Los
Huevos

Walk 37

3718m
El Teide

3550m

3270m

Pista a Montaña Blanca

Walk 37

Mirador
Pico Viejo

3480m

Station

**Montaña
Blanca**
2748m

Walk 37

N

0   1
          km

SF

Teleférico del Teide

Montaña
car p

Station

to Parador

*The path between
Montaña Blanca and
El Teide is flanked by
rugged, black lava flows*

**Montaña
Majúa**
2319m

from the lava
flows seen higher
up the mountain,
and have rolled down

the slopes to where they now rest. When a junction is reached, El Teide rises directly ahead, while a left turn leads gently onto **Montaña Blanca**, at 2748m (9016ft). The detour to the summit takes only a few minutes and is easily accomplished. It offers better views of El Teide, including the summit cone, than are available at closer quarters.

to El Portillo

to Puerto de la Cruz

The path climbing the eastern flank of El Teide is steep and unremitting, and it cannot be rushed. It is a dusty gravelly path that zigzags tightly and endlessly, hemmed in on either side by long, steep dark tongues of lava. Looking towards the skyline, the summit cannot be seen, but a slender post might be noticed which marks the position of a refuge. A few more 'Eggs of Teide' are passed and the path zigzags on a slope of gravel, boulders and broom. The path crosses a slope of reddish lava and is often on bare rock as it climbs further. There is little vegetation as the path gets close to the **Refugio Altavista**, which stands at 3270m (10,730ft). The

The Refugio Altavista offers basic accommodation and stands at 3270m (10,730ft) on El Teide

An evening view from the Refugio Altavista down to Montaña Blanca and Las Cañadas

paved area in front of it offers the chance to take a break on a level surface and admire extensive views east. ▸

The path climbing beyond the refuge is gravelly underfoot and flanked by masses of blocky lava. An old ice cave lies to the right. Further uphill the path is very uneven, being made of compacted boulders, but it is much easier than the huge angular blocks of lava to either side. The path climbs through a rocky defile and eventually reaches a junction with another path, Sendero 11. It is worth detouring to the right, where the path soon reaches the **Mirador La Fortaleza**, around 3550m (11,645ft). Fumaroles vent steam and sulphurous gases from the mountainside. ▸

The path, known as La Rambleta, wriggles around the bouldery upper slopes, up and down steps, reaching another junction just before the **teleférico station**. This path is the Telesforo Brava, Sendero 10, used for the final climb to the summit cone, and its use is controlled. Unless you aim to climb to the peak before dawn, you will need a permit, which must be shown to the person on duty. The path is obvious, stone-paved and zigzagging, climbing onto a cone that has only existed since 1798. Chains flank the path towards the top and there are fumaroles venting hot gases. There is no access to the crater, so keep picking a way along the path and finally scramble over blocks of rock to reach the summit of **El Teide** at 3718m (12,198ft).

For the descent there are a number of options. The easiest descent is of course via the *teleférico*, if it is running. If not, then either retrace your steps, bearing in mind that Walk 29 can be followed to El Portillo or, alternatively, descend by reversing Walk 38, which can be varied halfway down by switching to Walk 39.

If staying here overnight, note that the summit is almost 3km (2 miles) distant and another 500m (1640ft) above, where the air is noticeably thinner.

The rare *Gnaphalium teydeum* is one of the few plants able to survive such a hostile location.

WALK 38
El Teide via Pico Viejo

Start/Finish	Mirador de Chío
Distance	25km (15½ miles) there and back
Total Ascent/Descent	1700m (5575ft)
Time	10hrs
Terrain	A long and difficult climb, first on slopes of ash and pumice, and later on steeper slopes of rugged lava, eventually reaching the summit cone.
Refreshment	None
Transport	The Mirador de Chío is 3km (2 miles) off a bus route at Boca de Tauce.
Waymarked route(s)	Route uses Senderos 9, 10 and 12.

This is a long and difficult climb, taking in Pico Viejo as well as El Teide. There are great swathes of volcanic ash and pumice, as well as steep and rugged lava flows at a higher level. If the whole route seems too much, the climb to and from Pico Viejo is splendid in its own right.

The path to Pico Viejo winds around gentle slopes of stones, pumice and ash

There is a paved car park and viewpoint at **Mirador de Chío**, at almost 2100m (6890ft). The path is marked as Sendero 9 and while it starts level, it is rough and stony underfoot. It runs parallel to the road at first, heading roughly north-west, but later drifts away from the road and passes a lonesome pine. The path drops as it winds about, reaching a pine forest and joining a track. Follow the track onwards, but on emerging into the open, turn right up a narrow, dusty ash path flanked by parallel lines of stones. This winds up between broom and other scrub on jagged lava flows, eventually passing crude drystone structures.

The path swings right to climb through a valley, and is easy underfoot despite the ruggedness of the ground on **Lomo de Chío**. Towards the top of the valley, exit to the left across a barren slope of ash and pumice, overlooking several volcanic cones on the slopes heading towards the Teno peninsula. Zigzag up an ash path into a gentle crater at **Hoya de los Gazapos**, where hardly anything grows. Keep climbing and winding uphill, overlooking a crater and noting how the ground changes from black to red, over and over. Climb higher for a sudden view of Boca de Tauce and the car park at Mirador de Chío. Traverse across the slope, losing height for a while before climbing again. Soft ash and chunky pumice on this black slope prove slow and difficult.

Pass between a dark lower crater and a bright higher one, with remarkable colours at **Las Narices del Teide**, over 2650m (8695ft). ▶ The path heads downhill a bit and almost disappears, but a Sendero 9 marker shows a left turn uphill. Climb towards great rugs of broom where the path splits and it is not easy to pick the correct route. Going too far left leads off-route, while other paths are on soft ash, broken rock or solid rock. There is a rising zigzag traverse to the right, at a gentler gradient, but with more broom and rugged underfoot. Views over the gravel-strewn plains of Las Cañadas are particularly extensive, giving way to a long line of mountains. Keep climbing, and while roughly contouring, the summit cone of El Teide comes into view.

These craters are literally the 'nostrils' of Teide, which last 'blew' in 1798.

Pico Viejo's huge crater is best seen from high on the rugged slopes of El Teide

The vegetation runs out completely and spur paths head up to the left towards the crater rim on **Pico Viejo**. If taking these, follow a path along the eastern crater rim to climb to the highest point, at 3135m (10,285ft). This is the second highest peak on Tenerife and there are dramatic views of the

El Calderón

Lomo de Chío

Hoya de los Gazapos

Lomo Amarillo

to Guía de Isora

Walk 38

Mirador de Chío

crater. Bear in mind that there is absolutely no access to the crater. Either double back to the main path for El Teide, or look down the slope to spot other paths offering a short-cut.

The path reaches a broad col between Pico Viejo and El Teide, at around 3080m (10,105ft), covered in orange gravel. Watch for a path junction here, among broom scrub, where a right turn downhill reveals Sendero 23, which can be used to descend to the Roques de García and the Parador. ▶ Keeping left, however, leads gently uphill on light-coloured gravelly pumice, or *jable*. Nothing grows on these slopes and the path is often soft and loose. Pass some black boulders, then climb up a steep and rugged black lava flow. The path actually crosses a rugged barranco-like gash in the lava, then climbs

See map for Walk 39.

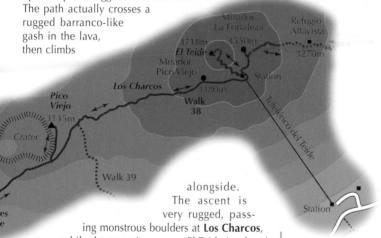

alongside. The ascent is very rugged, passing monstrous boulders at **Los Charcos**, while the summit cone on El Teide is often in view. This is the slowest and most tiring part of the ascent, but eventually it reaches the **Mirador Pico Viejo**, at 3104m (10,184ft), and a much easier path called La Rambleta or Sendero 12.

Follow the undulating, walled stone-paved path past fumaroles venting steam and sulphurous gases, to reach the **teleférico station**. Pass in front of the station and pass in front of an adjacent building. Turn left along a path called the Telesforo Brava, Sendero 10, which is used for the final climb to the summit cone. Its use is controlled, and unless you aim to climb to the peak before dawn, you will need a permit, which must be shown to the person on duty. The path is obvious, stone-paved and zigzagging, climbing onto a cone that has only existed since 1798. Chains flank the path towards the top and there are fumaroles venting hot gases. There is no access to the crater, so keep picking a way along the path and finally scramble over blocks of rock to reach the summit of **El Teide** at 3718m (12,198ft).

For the descent there are a number of options. The easiest descent is of course via the *teleférico*, if it is running. If not, then either retrace your steps, bearing in mind that the route can be varied halfway down by switching to Walk 39 or, alternatively, descend by reversing Walk 37, which leads past the Refugio Altavista if the night is to be spent on the mountain. The onward descent can be varied halfway down by switching to Walk 29 to El Portillo.

Walkers may need to wrap up warm on the rocky summit of El Teide

WALK 39
El Teide via Roques de García

Start/Finish	Parador
Distance	22km (13½ miles) there and back
Total Ascent/Descent	1600m (5250ft)
Time	8hrs
Terrain	An easy and well-trodden path gives way to an initially vague path, becoming steep and rugged as height is gained on the mountain.
Refreshment	Cafeteria los Roques at the Parador.
Transport	Buses serve the Parador from Playa de Las Américas, Los Cristianos, Vilaflor and Puerto de la Cruz.
Waymarked route(s)	Route uses Senderos 3, 9, 10, 12 and 23.

The Roques de García are immensely popular, but the ascent of El Teide from them is rarely used. However, Sendero 23 climbs towards the gap between Pico Viejo and El Teide, linking with Sendero 9 that can be used to climb higher. There are options to link with other routes for the descent.

The **Parador**, its café and the adjacent Visitor Centre stand at around 2150m (7055ft). Walk away from the hotel, past a chapel, to cross the main road and continue along a road that is virtually a linear car park. The end of the road can get very busy as people mill around viewpoints, climbing up and down stone steps; national park staff strive to keep people on the correct side of roped-off areas as people struggle to take photographs of the **Roques de García**. There are plenty of interpretative notices to study.

Leave the road-end viewpoint and turn right along a level path past one of the most striking pinnacles, the contorted and undercut, top-heavy **Roque Cinchado**. Continue along the foot of the rocks, gently rising and winding to about 2200m (7220ft), where there is a view of the whole southern flank of El Teide. As the light-coloured pinnacles of **Torre Blanco** are approached, watch out

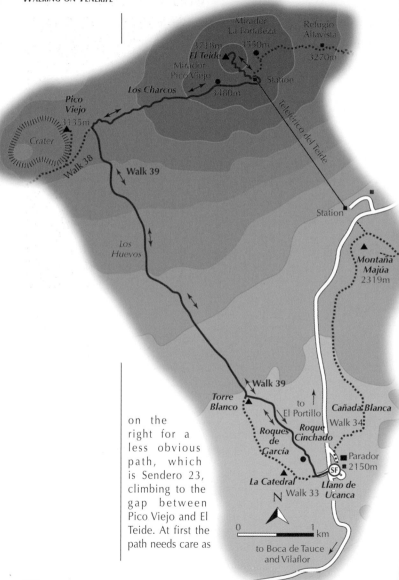

on the
right for a
less obvious
path, which
is Sendero 23,
climbing to the
gap between
Pico Viejo and El
Teide. At first the
path needs care as

it is often difficult to trace across an old, bare, crystalline lava flow.

Light-coloured pumice gives way to rugged black lava on the climb to El Teide

The path is better trodden as it climbs up a rugged scrubby slope onto another lava flow. However, step down from this later, turning right to climb further. The path is fairly easy, but becomes steeper and more rugged. Pass several huge, round dark boulders on another easy stretch. These are *Los Huevos del Teide*, or 'Eggs of Teide', lumps of lava that have become detached from the lava flows seen higher up the mountain, and have rolled down the slopes to where they now rest. Climb a snout of lava where the path is rugged and dusty, passing a marker for Sendero 23. Views open up well as height is gained and a winding sandy path continues uphill. There is a short descent before a massive round boulder is passed. Continue up a rugged path on lava, later passing broom and gnarled rock before another winding sandy path leads up to a junction on light-coloured gravelly pumice, or *jable*.

By diverting left, paths can be found climbing towards the crater rim on Pico Viejo.

The path reaches a broad col between **Pico Viejo** and El Teide, around 3080m (10,105ft). ◀ Turn right to continue along Sendero 9.

Climb gently uphill on the *jable*, where nothing grows and the path is often soft and loose. Pass some black boulders, then climb up a steep and rugged black lava flow. The path actually crosses a rugged barranco-like gash in the lava, then climbs alongside. The ascent is very rugged, passing monstrous boulders at **Los Charcos**, while the summit cone on El Teide is often in view. This is the slowest and most tiring part of the ascent, but eventually it reaches the **Mirador Pico Viejo**, at 3104m (10,184ft), and a much easier path called La Rambleta or Sendero 12.

Follow the undulating, walled and stone-paved path past fumaroles venting steam and sulphurous gases, to reach the **teleférico station**. Pass in front of the station and pass in front of an adjacent building. Turn left along a path called the Telesforo Brava, Sendero 10, which is used for the final climb to the summit cone. Its use is controlled, and unless you aim to climb to the peak before dawn, you will need a permit, which must be shown to

The author on El Teide at sunrise, when the mountain casts its shadow across the 'sea of clouds'

the person on duty. The path is obvious, stone-paved and zigzagging, climbing onto a cone that has only existed since 1798. Chains flank the path towards the top and there are fumaroles venting hot gases. There is no access to the crater, so keep picking a way along the path and finally scramble over blocks of rock to reach the summit of **El Teide** at 3718m (12,198ft).

For the descent there are a number of options. The easiest descent is of course via the *teleférico*, if it is running. If not, then either retrace your steps, bearing in mind that the route can be varied part-way down by switching to Walk 38. Alternatively, descend by reversing Walk 37, which leads past the Refugio Altavista if the night is to be spent on the mountain. The onward descent can be varied halfway down by switching to Walk 29 to El Portillo.

WALK 40
The Three Peaks of Tenerife

Start	Parador
Finish	Montaña Blanca car park
Distance	32km (20 miles)
Total Ascent	2300m (7545ft)
Total Descent	2100m (6890ft)
Time	15hrs
Terrain	A steep, rugged and rocky ascent, with a danger of rock-fall, followed by a rugged descent, with easier paths on the lower parts. On the next ascent, an initially vague path becomes steep and rugged as height is gained on the mountain. Note that there is a small risk of altitude sickness. A steep, rugged winding path is used for the descent, linking with a broad and easy vehicle track.
Refreshment	Cafeteria los Roques at the Parador.
Transport	Buses serve the Parador and Montaña Blanca car park from Playa de Las Américas, Los Cristianos, Vilaflor, El Portillo and Puerto de la Cruz.
Waymarked route(s)	Route uses Senderos 3, 4, 5, 9, 10, 12, 15, 23 and 31.

The three highest mountains on Tenerife are also the three highest mountains in the whole Canary Islands archipelago. They are close enough together to offer a splendid challenge for fit, tough and experienced walkers. Guajara is climbed first, followed by Pico Viejo, and finally El Teide.

The Parador, the rugged north face of Guajara, and the gaps on either side of the summit

Face the **Parador**, around 2150m 7055ft), and head to the right through a turning area to follow a path past a national park notice-board. The stony path is Sendero 4, running down a gentle slope covered in broom and other scrub. Cross a track and climb a stony path through scrub, noticing prominent tajinaste and a scattering of pines. This path is Sendero 31, climbing onto a gap next to a hill formed of yellow rock. Walk up a blunt ridge past broom, apparently heading for a wall of rock on the skyline ahead.

When the path reaches the rock wall it is pushed up to the right, later swinging left down onto a gap,

Degollada de Ucanca, at 2414m (7920ft). Guajara towers above, so continue towards it, climbing and winding, steep and stony, rocky and scrubby. The path is pushed to the left up a rising traverse below huge cliffs. Some parts are trodden dusty and white, and there are black boulders of obsidian lying around. The traverse gives way to a bouldery scramble to the summit of **Guajara**, at 2715m (8907ft). There is a square stone-walled enclosure on top, while views face Pico Viejo, El Teide and Montaña Blanca. ▸

Look across the sea to spot the islands of Gran Canaria, El Hierro, La Gomera and La Palma.

To leave the summit use Sendero 15, following a path gently downhill, roughly eastwards. It starts zigzagging and becomes gritty, dusty and white underfoot. Keep left at junctions to continue down stony and rocky slopes, undulating to reach a gap at 2373m (7785ft) on **Degollada de Guajara**. A large notice-board is reached at a path junction. Turn left down Sendero 5, which is plain and obvious once located. Although stony and narrow, on a rocky scrubby slope, it is fairly easy and leads unerringly down to a notice-board beside a clear track near the broad **Cañada del Montón de Trigo**, around 2200m (7220ft).

Turn left to follow the track over a rise. Sendero 16 heads right, so keep straight ahead and follow the track downhill, later wriggling around pinnacles and buttresses while rising and falling. A rugged path offers a short-cut through one pronounced bend. A curiously eroded mass of yellow rock at the foot of Guajara is appropriately named **Piedras Amarillas**. Pass a stone cabin and watch for a path on the right, which leads directly back to the **Parador**, and was used earlier.

Walk away from the hotel, past a chapel, to cross the main road and continue along a road that is virtually a linear car park. Leave the road-end and turn right along a level path past one of the most striking pinnacles, the contorted and undercut, top-heavy **Roque Cinchado**. Continue along the foot of the rocks, gently rising and winding to about 2200m (7220ft), where there is a view of the whole southern flank of El Teide. As the light-coloured pinnacles of **Torre Blanco** are approached, watch out on the right for a less obvious path, which is Sendero 23,

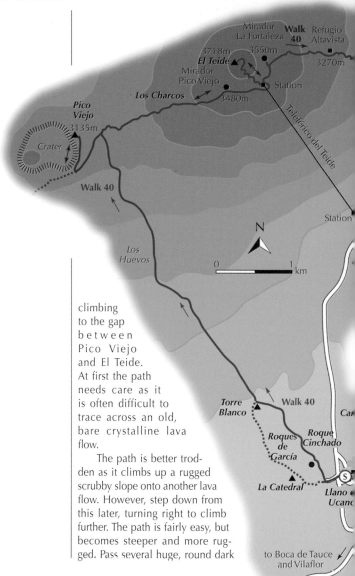

climbing
to the gap
b e t w e e n
Pico Viejo
and El Teide.
At first the path
needs care as it
is often difficult to
trace across an old,
bare crystalline lava
flow.

The path is better trod-
den as it climbs up a rugged
scrubby slope onto another lava
flow. However, step down from
this later, turning right to climb
further. The path is fairly easy, but
becomes steeper and more rugged. Pass several huge, round dark

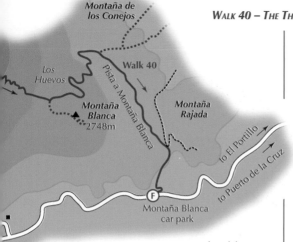

boulders on another easy stretch. These are *Los Huevos del Teide*, or 'Eggs of Teide', lumps of lava that have become detached from the lava flows seen higher up the mountain, and have rolled down the slopes to where they now rest. Climb a snout of lava where the path is rugged and dusty, passing a marker for Sendero 23. Views open up well as height is gained and a winding sandy path continues uphill. There is a short descent before a massive round boulder is passed. Continue up a rugged path on lava, later passing broom and gnarled rock before another winding sandy

Looking from Pico Viejo to El Teide, where paths vary from very easy to very difficult

path leads up to a junction on light-coloured gravelly pumice, or *jable*.

The path reaches a broad col between Pico Viejo and El Teide, around 3080m (10,105ft). Turn left and watch for a good path climbing on the right, leading to the crater rim on **Pico Viejo**. Keep right to follow a path along the eastern crater rim to climb to the highest point, at 3135m (10,285ft). Retrace your steps to the broad gap and use Sendero 9 to climb gently uphill on the *jable*, where nothing grows and the path is often soft and loose.

Pass some black boulders, then climb up a steep and rugged black lava flow. The path actually crosses a rugged barranco-like gash in the lava, then climbs alongside. The ascent is very rugged, passing monstrous boulders at **Los Charcos**, while the summit cone on El Teide is often in view. This is the slowest and most tiring part of the ascent, but eventually it reaches the **Mirador Pico Viejo**, at 3104m (10,184ft), and a much easier path called La Rambleta or Sendero 12.

Follow the undulating, walled and stone-paved path past fumaroles venting steam and sulphurous gases, to

reach the **teleférico station**. Pass in front of the station and pass in front of an adjacent building. Turn left along a path called the Telesforo Brava, Sendero 10, which is used for the final climb to the summit cone. Its use is controlled, so you will need a permit, which must be shown to the person on duty. The path is obvious, stone-paved and zigzagging, climbing onto a cone that has only existed since 1798. Chains flank the path towards the top and there are fumaroles venting hot gases. There is no access to the crater, so keep picking a way along the path and finally scramble over blocks of rock to reach the summit of **El Teide** at 3718m (12,198ft).

The summit of El Teide is the highest Spanish mountain, at 3718m (12,198ft)

Either retrace your steps to the *teleférico* station for a rapid descent if it is running, or turn left before it along the path called La Rambleta, Sendero 11. This wriggles around bouldery upper slopes, up and down steps, reaching a junction. ▶ Turn right down Sendero 7, which has huge angular blocks of lava to either side and later drops through a rocky defile. The path becomes gravelly and easier as it approaches the **Refugio Altavista**, at 3270m (10,730ft). The paved area in front

A short walk ahead leads to Mirador La Fortaleza, around 3550m (11,645ft), where fumaroles vent steam and sulphurous gases.

193

A light-coloured pumice path leads to rugged black lava on the climb to El Teide

Walk 29 joins here, offering a descent to El Portillo.

of the refuge offers an opportunity to take a break on a level surface.

The path continues downhill and crosses bare rock and a slope of reddish lava, then zigzags down a slope of gravel, boulders and broom, dusty and gravelly underfoot, hemmed in on either side by long, steep dark tongues of lava. Eventually the path levels out and a junction is reached with a track. **Montaña Blanca** lies straight ahead, at 2748m (9016ft), easily reached by a short detour. To continue the descent, however, turn left down the track, which is very bendy and dusty, almost white where vehicles run along it, but flanked by pale yellow slopes of gravelly pumice, or *jable*.

During the descent many huge, round dark boulders are passed. These are *Los Huevos del Teide*, or 'Eggs of Teide', lumps of lava that have become detached from the lava flows seen higher up the mountain, and have rolled down the slopes to where they now rest. A large sign stands on the left at almost 2550m (8365ft). ◄ Staying on the track, the descent is gentler and the track eventually reaches the Montaña Blanca **car park**, around 2350m (7710ft). Either aim to arrive in time for a bus, or arrange a pick-up by car.

GR 131 – ARONA TO LA ESPERANZA

The GR 131 climbs high through the mountains of Tenerife on its way from Arona to La Esperanza

The GR 131 is an evolving long-distance trail across all seven of the Canary Islands, linking with the pan-European E7 route. The route is fully signposted and waymarked across the small islands of La Palma, El Hierro and La Gomera. In this guidebook the route is described as it continues across Tenerife. The route can be split wherever lodgings or bus services are available, and it can be covered in five days.

The first day from Arona climbs past old cultivation terraces and rugged little mountains, crossing barrancos and winding up into pine forests. It drops down to the mountain village of Vilaflor. The second day climbs from Vilaflor, through extensive pine forest, emerging on barren slopes of black ash on the flanks of Guajara. It enters the amazing Parque Nacional del Teide, where the only lodging is at the Parador hotel. An easy and almost level stage runs across gravelly plains, surrounded by mountains, to reach El Portillo. There is nowhere to stay, but there are bus services. The fourth day is largely downhill, through pine and laurisilva forest, reaching La Caldera. Again, there is no accommodation, but there are regular bus services. The final day is long and quite convoluted, wandering through pine and laurisilva forest, finally emerging at the village of La Esperanza near La Laguna.

The GR 131 is planned to continue across Gran Canaria, Fuerteventura and Lanzarote, offering an exciting and interesting island-hopping long-distance trek.

WALK 41

GR 131 – Arona to Vilaflor

Start	Plaza Cristo de la Salud in Arona
Finish	Iglesia de San Pedro, Vilaflor
Distance	20km (12½ miles)
Total Ascent	1400m (4595ft)
Total Descent	400m (1310ft)
Time	8hrs
Terrain	Steep, stony scrubby slopes give way to forested slopes. Paths are usually clear and obvious, sometimes stony, with occasional short road-walks.
Refreshment	Bars in Arona. Bar at Ifonche. Bars in Vilaflor.
Transport	Regular daily buses serve Arona and Vilaflor from Playa de las Américas, Los Cristianos and Granadilla.

Paths used by the GR 131 to climb from Arona to Ifonche pass old cultivation terraces. The continuation of the route links with restored forest paths at a higher level. Vilaflor is the highest mountain village in the Canary Islands, and offers a good range of facilities.

Start in the village of **Arona** on the Plaza Cristo de la Salud, at around 630m (2065ft). There is a map-board behind the church and the walk starts by following a road, Calle San Carlos Borromeo, up out of town. Cross the main road and follow a road signposted for Roque del Conde. Climb past a house, La Casa del Pintor, around 650m (2130ft) at **Vento**, and walk downhill. Turn left down Calle Vento, then right between houses, where a stub of tarmac road and a track give way to stone steps down into a barranco.

Climb uphill and cross a rocky scrubby slope featuring prickly pears, tabaibal, verode, cardón, lavender and rushes. ◄ Watch for a path climbing on the right, flanked by stones, crossing a concrete water channel and a pipe. The path continues to be flanked by stones, with

Walk 16 continues straight ahead for Roque del Conde.

a fenced edge where it over-looks the **Barranco del Rey**. Keep well to the left of a building and drop easily into the barranco before reaching a ruin at **Ancón**.

Climb steps and follow an easy path flanked by stones and scrub. Keep left of a ruined build-ing and a circular *era*, or threshing floor, and note a well down to the left. The path climbs and drifts left, winding up through a valley to reach a gap, **Degollada de los Frailes**, below Roque del Conde. There is a view over the edge to Adeje, and the islands of La Gomera and La Palma can be seen across the sea.

Map continues on page 200

Benitez

Ifonche

Bar

Montaña Carasco 1034m

N

0   1 km

Walk 41

Montaña de los Brezos

El Refugio

Ruin

Roque Imoque 1112m

Barranco de Fañabe

Casa del Topo

Casa de Suárez

Barranco del Rey

Degollada de los Frailes

Res

Ancón

La Granja

Roque del Conde 1001m

Las Casas

ARONA

Vento

Walk 41

Barranco del Rey

La Centinela

to *Los Cristianos*

Turn right and follow a path hacked from ash and pumice on the slopes of Montaña de Suárez. The summit rises to 834m (2736ft) but the path keeps below it, crossing a gentle gap near **Casa de Suárez**, where there is a stone water channel and an *era*. Climb again towards the prominent tower-like **Roque Imoque**. The path keeps well below the summit, with a fenced edge as it reaches a gap at the head of **Barranco de Fañabe**. ▶ A splendid *era* sits on the gap, and the path passes it on the left. Aim to the left of

The summit of Roque Imoque can be gained by a steep climb and a rocky scramble; see Walk 17.

A fenced stretch of the GR 131 reaches a gap below the prominent Roque Imoque

Walk 18 crosses here, from La Escalona to Adeje. ◄

a nearby house, Finca Pastor Oliva, and turn left up its access road.

The road crosses the slopes of **Montaña de los Brezos**, reaching a gap among sparse pines and cistus over 1000m (3280ft). There are views on the left, down into a barranco. Stay on the road and keep straight ahead at junctions to reach a crossroads at the Restaurante El Dornajo in **Ifonche**. A left turn is signposted for the Barranco del Infierno, while a right turn leads to La Escalona. ◄

Follow a narrow road uphill from the bar, and keep right when the road forks. Keep right again up a track flanked by street lights, cross a hump, then watch for a path heading down to the right, flanked by stones. This leads into pine forest and crosses the bed of a barranco, where the ground cover is tagasaste, cistus and rock rose.

Follow the path uphill and it becomes aligned to a well-defined rocky ridge in the forest. Later it drifts well to the left of the ridge and climbs a flight of stone steps. Zigzags take it up onto a broad and stony crest where the pines thin out and the gradient is usually easier. An

era lies to the right, then later watch as the path drops to the right down to the bed of **Barranco del Rey**, where the altitude is around 1400m (4595ft).

The path climbs from the barranco, levels out, then falls gently. Always keep to the clearest path, which is usually flanked by stones, first drifting away from the barranco, then turning right down a broad and stony forested crest. Again, watch for the path as it suddenly swings left and winds down towards a terraced slope. White painted arrows and blobs mark the route as it passes between terraces, climbs past a small reservoir, then drops towards the edge of a field.

The path crosses a fine stone bridge over the **Barranco del Cuervo**, then has a fenced edge as it climbs. Fork left and climb across a track. The path winds uphill close to a series of terraces and eventually reaches a track on a broad gritty gap behind **Montaña Mohino**. Follow the track gently uphill, then gently down a little past terraces, to reach an intersection of tracks.

Walk straight ahead up a rugged track, and just before reaching a mass of pipes and a few terraces, turn left up a

Forest tracks and paths are linked high above Ifonche and the Barranco del Rey

199

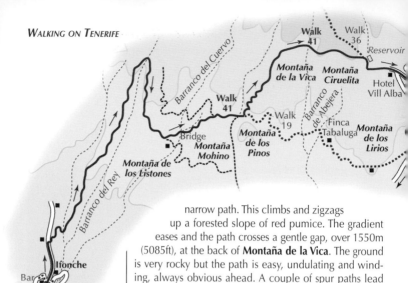

narrow path. This climbs and zigzags up a forested slope of red pumice. The gradient eases and the path crosses a gentle gap, over 1550m (5085ft), at the back of **Montaña de la Vica**. The ground is very rocky but the path is easy, undulating and winding, always obvious ahead. A couple of spur paths lead left towards circular enclosures with low walls. The path crosses a bouldery streambed close to where the stream leaps over a cliff into the **Barranco de Abejera**.

Follow the path onwards and uphill, around a big rocky bluff. The highest point of the day's walk is gained, around 1600m (5250ft). A water pipe runs beside the path, which drops gently towards a covered **reservoir**. Walk down the rugged access track and keep left at a junction, down through forest, levelling out to pass through a cultivated area. Another short stretch through

A stone bridge is crossed over the Barranco del Cuervo before climbing to Montaña Mohino

forest leads to a road-end between a football pitch and **Hotel Vill Alba**.

Pass the hotel and keep left at a fork in the road. The Ermita San Roque has a small plaza offering a fine view of Vilaflor. Walk down a stone-paved path and steps beside the road. Cross the main road and follow Calle Los Molinos down into **Vilaflor**, reaching the church of San Pedro and its plaza, around 1465m (4805ft).

WALK 42
GR 131 – Vilaflor to Parador

Start	Iglesia de San Pedro, Vilaflor
Finish	Parador
Distance	18km (11 miles)
Total Ascent	1060m (3480ft)
Total Descent	375m (1230ft)
Time	6hrs
Terrain	Clear paths throughout on slopes that are forested, ash-covered or rocky. After a rugged descent an easy track is used towards the finish.
Refreshment	Bars in Vilaflor. Cafeteria los Roques at the Parador.
Transport	Daily buses serve Vilaflor and the Parador from Playa de las Américas and Los Cristianos. The Parador is also served by bus from Puerto de la Cruz.

The GR 131 uses the ancient Camino de Chasna beyond Vilaflor. This route climbs through pine forest, emerging on slopes of volcanic ash. The path crosses a rocky gap beside Guajara and drops into the Parque Nacional del Teide. A spur leads to the Parador, the only place offering lodgings.

Start below the church of San Pedro in **Vilaflor**, around 1465m (4805ft). There is a map-board at the bottom of the plaza. Walk down a road and turn left, down and up Calle El Canario. Turn right down another road, then left after a house, as signposted along a stone-paved path. A rugged path drops into the terraced **Barranco del Chorillo**. Cross its bed as flashed red/yellow/white, for both the GR 131 and PR TF 72. Follow a track uphill, then turn right up a narrower walled path, which becomes a track.

The track is variously stony, rocky or stone-paved, climbing past pines and tagasaste. A water pipe runs alongside and the path is gentler as it passes a farm at **Galindo**, where there are concrete terraces on the left and almonds on the right. Climb further and turn right at the top. Walk down a narrow path that becomes a broad stone-paved path down into the **Barranco de las Mesas**. Tajinaste grows in the bed of the barranco, and the path climbs to a forest road.

Turn right and quickly left as signposted, climbing up stone steps to continue along the path. A three-way signpost is reached, where the PR TF 72 heads left and

Map continues on page 204

The path climbs towards Guajara on soft volcanic ash and is flanked by parallel lines of stones

right, while the GR 131 heads only left. It is possible to follow the trail to the right, re-joining the GR 131 above the *Paisaje Lunar*. ▶ The path winds up a rocky stony slope, passing a big pine tree with stone seats alongside. Climbing higher, the path becomes easier and there are glimpses of Guajara towering above the pine forest.

Cross a narrow track and later cross a broad track. Go straight up past a barrier gate up a steep and stony track. This becomes gentler as it passes the ruins of **El Marrubial**. A steep and winding stretch later climbs through beds of crumbling, gravelly light-coloured pumice, or *jable*. The track is gentler again, crossing the bed of the **Barranco Erís del Carnero**, climbing past pines and broom to reach a junction.

Keep right, pass an old water channel and avoid another path climbing to the left. A signpost is reached around 2000m (6560ft), where there is a view back to the prominent Roque del Encaje. The PR TF 72 drops right, steeply and ruggedly, to a viewpoint for the nearby *Paisaje Lunar*. ▶ The GR 131 climbs left, steep and stony among pines, then up slopes of red and black volcanic

This would suit anyone wishing to use a remote campsite off-route at Madre del Agua.

See Walk 20.

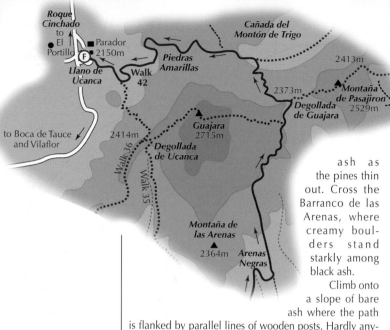

ash as the pines thin out. Cross the Barranco de las Arenas, where creamy boulders stand starkly among black ash.

Climb onto a slope of bare ash where the path is flanked by parallel lines of wooden posts. Hardly anything grows, but there are pines further downhill. Reach a junction where paths are marked by parallel lines of stones, and turn left uphill on soft and crunchy ash. The path appears to head straight for the summit of Guajara, while Gran Canaria can be seen floating on the 'sea of clouds'. Black ash gives way abruptly to creamy boulders short of 2400m (7875ft).

The path is trodden to gravel and dust and winds all over the slope, which bears sparse pines and clumps of flowery scrub. Without the path, progress would be dreadfully slow, but it climbs and contours fairly easily, drifting to the right and passing a solitary juniper bush. There is plenty of broom at a higher level and the path reaches a metal post at a junction. ◄ Keep straight ahead, down past crumbling *jable*, then the path undulates across a rocky slope to reach a gap, **Degollada de Guajara**, at 2373m (7785ft). This is the highest point reached on the GR 131 through Tenerife. Views include

The summit of Guajara can be reached by turning left on the well-trodden path.

The highest point on the GR 131 in Tenerife is on the Degollada de Guajara at 2373m (7785ft)

Guajara, Pico Viejo, El Teide, Montaña Blanca and nearby Montaña de Pasajiron.

Watch for a path heading downhill, which is plain and obvious once located. Although stony and narrow, on a rocky scrubby slope, it is fairly easy and leads unerringly down to a notice-board beside a clear track near the broad **Cañada del Montón de Trigo**, at around 2200m (7220ft). The GR 131 turns right to reach El Portillo, but the only lodging available is at the Parador, which is reached by turning left.

So, turn left to follow the track over a rise. Sendero 16 heads right, but keep ahead and follow the track downhill, later wriggling around pinnacles and buttresses, while rising and falling. A rugged path offers a short-cut through one pronounced bend. A curiously eroded mass of yellow rock at the foot of Guajara is appropriately named **Piedras Amarillas**. Pass a stone cabin and watch for a path on the right, Sendero 4. This leads directly to the **Parador**, Cafeteria Los Roques and a little Visitor Centre dispensing information about the Parque Nacional del Teide, all around 2150m (7055ft).

WALK 43

GR 131 – Parador to El Portillo

Start	Parador
Finish	El Portillo
Distance	17km (10½ miles)
Total Ascent	200m (655ft)
Total Descent	250m (820ft)
Time	5hrs
Terrain	An easy and gently undulating gravel track flanked by exceptionally rugged ground.
Refreshment	Cafeteria los Roques at the Parador. Bar at El Portillo.
Transport	Daily buses serve El Portillo and the Parador from Playa de las Américas, Los Cristanos, Vilaflor and Puerto de la Cruz.

This is an easy stretch of the GR 131, and a popular day's walk in its own right. A clear track is followed past a series of level gravel *cañadas* with jagged lava snouts to the left and rugged mountains to the right. El Teide looms large, but remains distant, throughout the walk.

Start at the turning space beside the **Parador**, beside the national park Visitor Centre, at 2150m (7055ft). Follow a marked path, Sendero 4, gently down across a scrubby slope towards Guajara, Turn left along a clear track past a stone cabin. Ahead is a curiously eroded mass of yellow rock at the foot of Guajara, appropriately named **Piedras Amarillas**. While following the track onwards and uphill, note that it makes a pronounced bend, which can be cut short using a rugged path climbing on the right.

The track descends, passing pinnacles and rock buttresses, then rises to 2200m (7220ft). On the way downhill Sendero 16 heads left, but keep straight ahead along Sendero 4. A notice on the right marks the start of Sendero 5 to Guajara. Tall tajinaste are prominent on the rocky slopes, flourishing since grazing was banned in the national park. Follow the track past **Cañada del Montón de Trigo**, which holds water after heavy rain, or whenever snow melts.

Map continues on page 208

The track rises gently and runs down a valley where the slopes are thick with tajinaste. Walk past the narrow, boulder-strewn Cañada de la Carnellita, with the

207

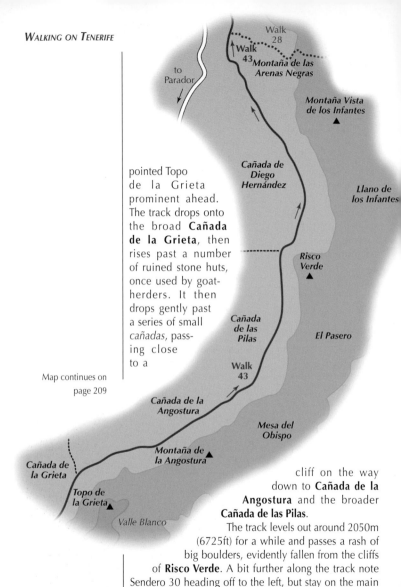

pointed Topo de la Grieta prominent ahead. The track drops onto the broad **Cañada de la Grieta**, then rises past a number of ruined stone huts, once used by goatherders. It then drops gently past a series of small *cañadas*, passing close to a

Map continues on page 209

cliff on the way down to **Cañada de la Angostura** and the broader **Cañada de las Pilas**.

The track levels out around 2050m (6725ft) for a while and passes a rash of big boulders, evidently fallen from the cliffs of **Risco Verde**. A bit further along the track note Sendero 30 heading off to the left, but stay on the main track, rising gently uphill through the broad **Cañada de**

Diego Hernández. The track levels out, then undulates past rough and rocky hummocks, with gentle hollows of light-coloured gravelly pumice, or *jable*, in between.

Sendero 2 heads off to the right for Arenas Negras (used on Walk 28), but keep ahead along the track. Bare black ash rises to the right later, then there is dense scrub on the way down to a barrier gate. As the track runs downhill Sendero 2 joins from the right. Cross a broad dip of bare *jable* and make a short climb to the main road, at around 2050m (6725ft).

The national park **Visitor Centre** lies across the road. Turn right down the road, walking on the left-hand side for safety, to reach **El Portillo** at 1980m (6495ft). ▶

Alto de Guamasa ▲

Restaurante El Portillo **F** to La Laguna →

Visitor Centre

Walk 28

Montaña El Cerrillar 2346m ▲

Restaurants

Walk 28

↑Walk 43 *Montaña de las Arenas Negras*

to Parador

There is no accommodation, but a bar–restaurant offers food and drink and buses stop on the road alongside.

An easy and mostly level track runs through Las Cañadas, passing below Topo de la Grieta

209

WALK 44

GR 131 – El Portillo to La Caldera

Start	El Portillo
Finish	La Caldera
Distance	13km (8 miles)
Total Ascent	300m (985ft)
Total Descent	1100m (3610ft)
Time	4hrs 30mins
Terrain	Mostly clear winding forest paths, intersecting with or following forest tracks.
Refreshment	Bar at El Portillo. Bar at La Caldera.
Transport	Daily buses serve El Portillo from Playa de las Américas, Los Cristianos, Vilaflor and Puerto de la Cruz. Regular daily buses serve La Caldera from Puerto de la Cruz.

This stretch of the trail is mostly downhill, mostly forested and mostly confined to the Parque Natural Corona Forestal. There are no facilties except for the bar restaurants and bus services at the start and finish. Views are limited and this area is notoriously misty.

Start at the restaurant at **El Portillo**, at 1980m (6495ft). Go to the far side of the big triangular road junction to find the start of Sendero 14. Walk down the path to reach a junction, where Sendero 14 turns right up to Alto de Guamasa (visited on Walk 27) while the GR 131 turns left downhill. Follow the dusty winding path down a scrubby slope, suddenly entering pine forest and briefly running level. The descent re-commences, rugged and winding alongside the **Barranco de la Raya**, eventually reaching a main road, at around 1800m (5905ft), where the route runs through a concrete **tunnel**.

Continue down the winding forest path and cross a track as marked. Further downhill there is a fine view of the barranco, as well as the wider Valle de la Orotava. The path is remarkably convoluted, with few reference points,

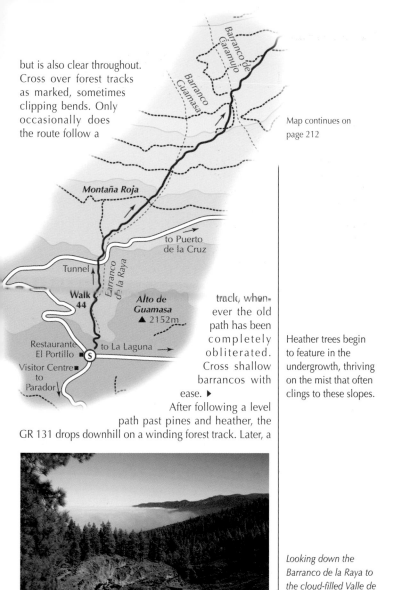

but is also clear throughout. Cross over forest tracks as marked, sometimes clipping bends. Only occasionally does the route follow a

Map continues on page 212

track, whenever the old path has been completely obliterated. Cross shallow barrancos with ease. ▶

After following a level path past pines and heather, the GR 131 drops downhill on a winding forest track. Later, a

Heather trees begin to feature in the undergrowth, thriving on the mist that often clings to these slopes.

Looking down the Barranco de la Raya to the cloud-filled Valle de la Orotava

211

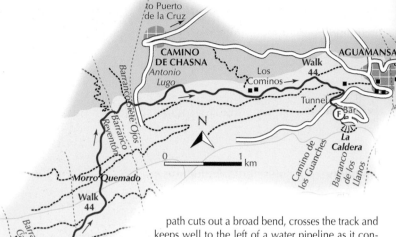

You may catch a glimpse of Puerto de la Cruz below.

path cuts out a broad bend, crosses the track and keeps well to the left of a water pipeline as it continues down beside the **Barranco de Caramujo**. Turn right to cross a shallow part of the barranco, at around 1325m (4350ft), cross the pipeline and later follow the path through an area where there is dense broom in the undergrowth. A slope is reached where many pines have been felled, leaving only a few tall ones standing. The ground is densely covered with young pines, heather trees, broom, tagasaste, cistus, rock rose and timber leftovers. Traverse this area on a gentle descent. ◄

Turn left down a rough and stony track, and go down through a cross-tracks as marked, on **Morro Quemado**. Keep straight ahead, down through all junctions as marked, through regenerating laurisilva forest and lush dense forest. When a cultivated slope is reached, swing right as marked down a track, and right at the next junction, beside a big pine tree, back into laurisilva forest.

Turn left down the next track and cross the wooded bed of **Barranco Reventón**, above 1000m (3280ft), climbing the short and steep route from it. Walk straight ahead along a terrace path and down a crumbling concrete road between cultivated plots, continuing straight ahead along a grassy track. Pass a sign for Cruz del Dornajito and go down log steps into laurisilva to cross the **Barranco Siete**

The Barranco de Caramujo is often flanked by cliffs with pines on top

A little white shrine is passed as the GR 131 crosses the Barranco Siete Ojos

Ojos, where the path passes between a shelter and a shrine.

Climb log steps to leave, and cross a steep road. Follow a path between bramble-tangled heather trees and laurisilva, roughly following a covered water channel at **Antonio Lugo**. Cross a track and continue, then cross the channel and go down log steps past a little covered reservoir. The path undulates through laurisilva with a water pipe alongside. Turn right up a concrete road and level out, turning steeply right up a track to another covered reservoir.

Turn left along a level track, past chestnuts, climbing again among heather trees and chestnuts, with a fence to the left. Follow the fence, which helps to reveal a path heading down to the left. Cross a streambed and climb, then undulate across a slope of thinned laurisilva. The path is always clear and is marked ahead. Part of it has a fence to the left, while most of it has a low tumble-down wall to the left. Cross another streambed and continue traversing through the laurisilva. Pass fences and note a couple of houses tucked away in the trees to the left around **Los Cominos**.

Reach a signpost and keep straight ahead beside another fence. Go down a track and cross a road-end to continue along another track. Watch for a signpost on the right for Aguamansa and climb steeply into laurisilva. Reach a track and turn left up through the woods. When the track turns right, keep straight ahead up a path to a junction. Turn right at another signpost and follow a path climbing parallel to the track, reaching another track. Cross over this and go through a concrete **tunnel** beneath the main road.

The 'caldera' itself is a deep hollow completely surrounded by woodland, with a play area and barbeque hearths in the middle.

There is a road junction here, and the GR 131 is marked and signposted from it, climbing and winding through the woods among tall pines and tall straggly heather trees. Stone steps climb to a car park and bus stop at **La Caldera**, at almost 1200m (2935ft). There are information boards detailing trails around this popular recreational area, and there is a bar restaurant nearby. ▶

WALK 45
GR 131 – La Caldera to La Esperanza

Start	La Caldera
Finish	La Esperanza
Distance	30km (18½ miles)
Total Ascent	1000m (3280ft)
Total Descent	1300m (4265ft)
Time	10hrs
Terrain	Almost entirely along forest tracks and paths, usually easy and gently graded, but sometimes steep. One path runs across cliffs and is quite exposed. There are several junctions with other paths and tracks.
Refreshment	Bar at La Caldera. Bars at La Esperanza.
Transport	Regular daily buses serve La Caldera from Puerto de la Cruz. Buses serve La Esperanza from La Laguna.

This is the longest stage of the GR 131 through Tenerife and it is almost entirely confined to laurisilva and pine forests, so views are limited. One stretch crosses steep and rocky slopes, but most of the paths and tracks, while convoluted and fiddly, are easy to walk.

Start at **La Caldera** and walk past the bar until a dirt road heads off to the left. A stout marker indicates the GR 131 and notes that it is also part of the trans-European E7. The broad dirt road is gentle and easy, passing pines, heather trees and bushy rock rose. Cross a bridge over a rocky forested barranco and reach a shelter at **Pero Gil**, where signposts indicate all sorts of routes. Keep following the dirt road and swing easily around another forested barranco. Rise slightly, then head generally downhill. Note how the trees are hung with long straggly lichen because of the moisture in the air. There is another slight rise and descent, and stone steps can be seen climbing on the right. Follow the dirt road past a stone-built house, **Casa del Agua**, at around 1150m (3775ft). ◄ Continue as signposted for the Camino El Topo, crossing a stone bridge over the **Barranco de la Madre**, rise gently, look round to see rocky buttresses towering above the forest and then fork right at a track junction.

Almost immediately, turn right up stone steps as signposted and

The Ruta del Agua, Walk 24, climbs up steps from the building.

Map continues on page 218

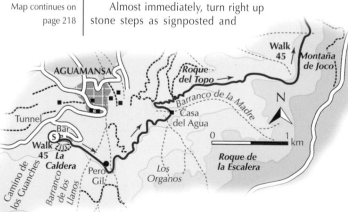

climb the steep forested slope towards **Roque del Topo**.
Cross a track and continue winding uphill, past a curved
stone seat. Level out a couple of times on the forested
crest and zigzag steeply up to a rocky outcrop and a
signposted path junction, at around 1550m (5085ft). Turn
left for the GR 131 (right is Walk 23), downhill at first,
followed by a long rising traverse across a steep, rocky
forested slope. There is a brief glimpse down to Puerto de
la Cruz. Continue climbing, then descend and undulate
while crossing a barranco, with splendid views straight
down to Puerto de la Cruz.

Climbing through dense pine forest, with a heather tree understorey, towards the Roque del Topo

Follow a rising traverse then zigzag, going through
a rocky cleft and zigzagging down into a dip. Zigzag
up through another rocky cleft and go round a corner
where there is a fence alongside. The path undulates and
enters the Paisaje Protegido La Resbala on the slopes
of **Montaña de Joco**. There are log steps and a lot more
fencing for security, plus an additional safety cable bolted
to rockfaces. The path eventually crosses a broad dirt
road and zigzags down flights of log steps among dense
pines and heather, far below the **Mirador de Chipeque**.

217

The path almost lands on a track, but traverses above it for a while, turning right to go gently down it later. Go up fenced steps to follow another stretch of path, rising gently and going down log steps, back onto a track at a junction on a bend.

Walk ahead as marked, down into dense forest, with a view down one forested barranco. An undulating traverse with some steps crunches across a forested slope of ash. Zigzag down and continue along a falling traverse to a signposted path junction. Keep right along a pleasant traverse where an abundance of old yellow diamond marker plates are nailed to trees,

Map continues on page 220

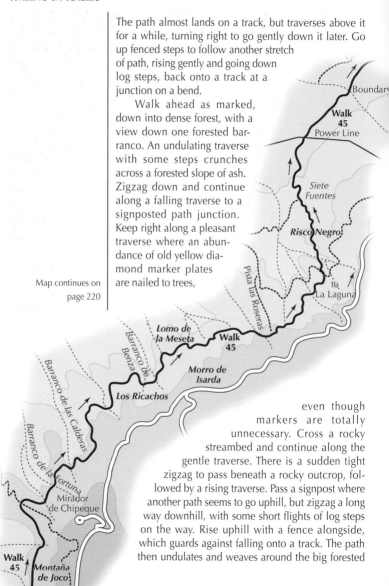

even though markers are totally unnecessary. Cross a rocky streambed and continue along the gentle traverse. There is a sudden tight zigzag to pass beneath a rocky outcrop, followed by a rising traverse. Pass a signpost where another path seems to go uphill, but zigzag a long way downhill, with some short flights of log steps on the way. Rise uphill with a fence alongside, which guards against falling onto a track. The path then undulates and weaves around the big forested

Barranco de Benza and is very mossy in places, with one glimpse down to the well-settled slopes near the sea.

Climb and cross the **Lomo de la Meseta**, traverse across a slope and turn round a little barranco. The path undulates and there are a few log steps crossing another little barranco. Zigzag up log steps, then undulate with a few more log steps up and down. A few steps drop to a streambed, then lots of steps zigzag up from it to a track. Cross over to continue along the path, rising, then climbing long flights of steps. Keep climbing and winding to reach a forest track, **Pista Las Roseras**, and a barrier gate. ▸

Cross the track and head downhill, zigzagging and turning round a couple of little barrancos. There is a glimpse down to La Matanza, easily identified by a little square reservoir. Traverse across a slope and go round and down through another little barranco. Leave to reach a forested crest, then swing right and zigzag down to a track. Turn left up the track for a short distance, then go down a path on the right. Cross another track and keep winding down into the bed of a barranco. Climb the other side, just as convoluted, and cross a track. ▸ The path continues and soon makes a series of tight zigzags on a

Keep your eyes peeled to spot red/white flashes through a network of forest tracks and paths

Turning right leads quickly to the main road, where this long day's walk could be broken, if a pick-up can be arranged.

All these barrancos feed into the Barranco del Rincón.

steep slope of pines and laurisilva. Cross a track and continue down the path. There are many more tight zigzags down to another track. Turn left and almost immediately right

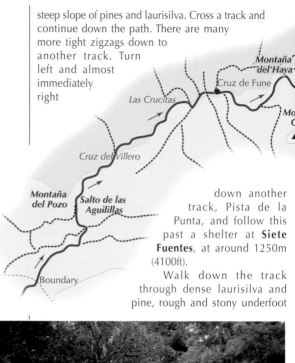

down another track, Pista de la Punta, and follow this past a shelter at **Siete Fuentes**, at around 1250m (4100ft).

Walk down the track through dense laurisilva and pine, rough and stony underfoot

A little shrine stands in dense forest at Cruz de Fune, on the way to La Esperanza

but gently graded. Avoid turnings and pass under a **power line**, catching a glimpse of Puerto de la Cruz. Rise gently and pass notices for the municipal **boundary** of La Victoria and La Matanza. Walk gently down the Pista de la Punta, through cut and replanted laurisilva, until signposted down to the left. A broad path runs down through the forest. Cross a track and continue down a broad and bendy path, which suddenly narrows in dense woods, winding down to another track. Turn right gently down this broad, red, clay track, which becomes gravelly in bramble-tangled woods. Pass a sign at **Salto de las Aguilillas**, and keep straight ahead at a track junction along the Pista las Aguilillas.

Pass notices for the municipal boundary of La Matanza and El Sauzal, and pass a sign at **Cruz del Villero**. The pines become tall and dense, with a bramble-tangled laurisilva understorey. Keep following the Pista las Aguilillas as it undulates gently onwards, reaching a clearer space with lots of bracken. Turn right at the end of the pista, at **Las Crucitas**, then turn left down Pista Fuente Fría, which bears a sign for Lomo la Jara. Walk down through dense laurisilva to a junction and turn right up Pista Cruz de Fune. Keep right of a little shrine at **Cruz de Fune**, up the Pista a La Esperanza. Climb to a junction, then walk ahead downhill, still signed as the Pista a La Esperanza, and still in dense forest of pines and laurisilva.

At the top of the next gentle rise, turn right at a crossroads, again signed as the Pista a La Esperanza, gently uphill. Follow the track up and around a wooded valley, where trees have been felled and replanted in parts. Reach a complex track junction and simply walk straight ahead along the clearest track. Pass eucalyptus trees and houses, and walk down a road to a roundabout. Go down Calle Grano de Oro to reach big paved squares and a full range of services and facilities in **La Esperanza**, at 900m (2950ft). Buses lead quickly to La Laguna for onward services.

Bear in mind that the GR 131 is an island-hopping route that crosses all seven of the Canary Islands. The continuation westwards across the small islands of La Palma, La Gomera and El Hierro is described in two other Cicerone guidebooks: *Walking on La Palma* and *Walking on La Gomera and El Hierro*. The continuation eastwards across the large islands of Gran Canaria, Fuerteventura and Lanzarote is described in two other Cicerone guidebooks: *Walking on Gran Canaria* and *Walking on Lanzarote and Fuerteventura*.

The trees in the forest are often hung with long straggly lichen

APPENDIX A

Route summary table

Walk	Start	Finish	Distance	Time	Total Ascent	Total Descent	Page
1	Pico del Inglés	La Quebrada or Valleseco, near Santa Cruz	7 or 9km (4½ or 5½ miles)	3hrs	30m (100ft)	960m (3150ft)	30
2	Igueste de San Andrés	Chamorga	10km (6¼ miles)	5hrs	875m (2870ft)	425m (1395ft)	33
3	Chamorga	Almáciga	16km (10 miles)	5hrs	300m (985ft)	800m (2625ft)	36
4	Almáciga	Almáciga	10km (6¼ miles)	3hrs	500m (1640ft)	500m (1640ft)	41
5	Taganana	Taganana	14km (8½ miles)	5hrs	1000m (3280ft)	1000m (3280ft)	43
6	Afur	Pico del Inglés	7km (4½ miles)	2hrs30	850m (2790ft)	50m (165ft)	48
7	Cruz del Carmen	Punta del Hidalgo	10km (6¼ miles)	3hrs30	50m (165ft)	1000m (3280ft)	51
8	Cruz del Carmen	Punta del Hidalgo	12km (7½ miles)	4hrs	250m (820ft)	1200m (3935ft)	55
9	Los Poleos	Los Poleos	6.5km (4 miles)	2hrs	150m (490ft)	150m (490ft)	61
10	Garachico	San José de los Llanos	17km (10½ miles)	6hrs	1400m (4595ft)	300m (985ft)	63
11	Santiago del Teide	Erjos	14km (8½ miles)	4hrs30	675m (2215ft)	575m (1885ft)	68
12	Erjos	Punta de Teno	20km (12½ miles)	7hrs	800m (2625ft)	1700m (5580ft)	72
13	Erjos	Masca	16km (10 miles)	5hrs	300m (985ft)	590m (1935ft)	77
14	Masca	Playa de Masca	4km (2½ miles)	2hrs	0m (0ft)	610m (2000ft)	81
15	Adeje	Adeje	7km (4½ miles)	3hrs	300m (985ft)	300m (985ft)	86

An aqueduct bridge spans a gorge deep in the Barranco de Valleseco (Walk 1)

Walk	Start	Finish	Distance	Time	Total Ascent	Total Descent	Page
16	Plaza Cristo de la Salud, Arona	Plaza Cristo de la Salud, Arona	7km (4½ miles)	3hrs	500m (1640ft)	500m (1640ft)	89
17	Plaza Cristo de la Salud, Arona	Plaza Cristo de la Salud, Arona	10km (6¼ miles)	3hrs30	450m (1475ft)	450m (1475ft)	91
18	La Escalona	Adeje	16km (10 miles)	5hrs	400m (1310ft)	1100m (3610ft)	95
19	Bus stop at Vilaflor	Bus stop at Vilaflor	10km (6¼ miles)	3hrs	350m (1150ft)	350m (1150ft)	99
20	Iglesia de San Pedro, Vilaflor	Iglesia de San Pedro, Vilaflor	13km (8 miles)	5hrs	500m (1640ft)	500m (1640ft)	102
21	Boca de Tauce	Chirche	15km (9½ miles)	5hrs	250m (820ft)	1450m (4760ft)	106
22	Aguamansa	Arafo	13km (8 miles)	5hrs	1020m (3345ft)	1545m (5070ft)	112
23	La Caldera	La Caldera	15km (9½ miles)	5hrs	600m (1970ft)	600m (1970ft)	116
24	La Caldera	La Caldera	8km (5 miles)	2hrs30	200m (655ft)	200m (655ft)	120
25	El Portillo	Realejo Alto	16km (10 miles)	5hrs	100m (330ft)	1800m (5905ft)	123
26	Mirador del Corral del Niño	Mirador del Corral del Niño	8km (5 miles)	2hrs30	200m (655ft)	200m (655ft)	129
27	El Portillo	El Portillo	4km (2½ miles)	1hr15	100m (330ft)	100m (330ft)	132
28	El Portillo	El Portillo	8km (5 miles)	2hrs30	100m (330ft)	100m (330ft)	134
29	El Portillo	El Portillo	22km (13½ miles)	7hrs	750m (2460ft)	750m (2460ft)	137
30	Km39 on the road east of El Portillo	Parador	21km (13 miles)	9hrs	475m (1560ft)	575m (1885ft)	140

The Barranco de Abejera above Vilaflor (Walk 19)

Walk	Start	Finish	Distance	Time	Total Ascent	Total Descent	Page
31	Parador	Parador	10km (6¼ miles)	4hrs	600m (1970ft)	600m (1970ft)	145
32	Parador	Parador	13km (8 miles)	5hrs	1000m (3280ft)	1000m (3280ft)	149
33	Parador	Parador	4km (2½ miles)	1hr30	150m (490ft)	150m (490ft)	153
34	Parador	Parador	11km (6¾ miles)	3hrs30	300m (985ft)	300m (985ft)	157
35	Parador	Iglesia de San Pedro, Vilaflor	15km (9½ miles)	6hrs	440m (1445ft)	1125m (3690ft)	161
36	Parador	Iglesia de San Pedro, Vilaflor	18km (11 miles)	7hrs	760m (2495ft)	1445m (4740ft)	166
37	Montaña Blanca car park	Montaña Blanca car park	20km (12½ miles)	9hrs	1400m (4595ft)	1400m (4595ft)	173
38	Mirador de Chío	Mirador de Chío	25km (15½ miles)	10hrs	1700m (5575ft)	1700m (5575ft)	178
39	Parador	Parador	22km (13½ miles)	8hrs	1600m (5250ft)	1600m (5250ft)	183
40	Parador	Montaña Blanca car park	32km (20 miles)	15hrs	2300m (7545ft)	2100m (6890ft)	187
41	Plaza Cristo de la Salud in Arona	Iglesia de San Pedro, Vilaflor	20km (12½ miles)	8hrs	1400m (4595ft)	400m (1310ft)	196
42	Iglesia de San Pedro, Vilaflor	Parador	18km (11 miles)	6hrs	1060m (3480ft)	375m (1230ft)	201
43	Parador	El Portillo	17km (10½ miles)	5hrs	200m (655ft)	250m (820ft)	206
44	El Portillo	La Caldera	13km (8 miles)	4hrs30	300m (985ft)	1100m (3610ft)	210
45	La Caldera	La Esperanza	30km (18½ miles)	10hrs	1000m (3280ft)	1300m (4265ft)	215

Rugged lava flows occur in many parts of Tenerife, such as this one meeting a cliff at Boca de Tauce (Walk 21)

APPENDIX B

Topographical glossary

Apart from a few place-names derived from original Guanche words, most names appearing on maps are Spanish. Many words appear frequently and are usually descriptive of landforms or colours. The following list of common words helps to sort out what some of the places on maps or signposts mean.

Spanish	English	Spanish	English
Agua	Water	Gordo/Gorda	Fat/Giant
Alto/Alta	High	Grande	Big
Arenas	Sands	Guagua	Bus
Arroyo	Stream	Hoya	Valley
Asomada	Promontory	Ladera	Slope
Bajo/Baja	Low	Llano	Plain
Barranco	Ravine	Lomo	Spur/Ridge
Barranquillo	Small Ravine	Montaña	Mountain
Blanco/Blanca	White	Morro	Nose
Boca	Gap	Negro/Negra	Black
Cabeza	Head	Nieve	Snow
Caldera	Crater	Nuevo/Nueva	New
Calle	Street	Parada	Bus Stop
Camino	Path/Track	Paso	Pass
Cañada	Gully	Pequeño/Pequeña	Small
Canal	Watercourse	Pico	Peak
Carretera	Road	Piedra	Rock
Casa	House	Pino/Pinar	Pine
Casa Forestal	Forestry House	Playa	Beach
Caseta	Small House/Hut	Plaza	Town Square
Collada/Degollada	Col/Gap/Saddle	Presa	Small Reservoir
Colorada	Coloured	Puerto	Port
Cruz	Cross/Crossroads	Punta	Point
Cueva	Cave	Risco	Cliff
Cumbre	Ridge/Crest	Rojo/Roja	Red
De/Del	Of/Of the	Roque	Rock
El/La/Los/Las	The	San/Santa	Saint (male/female)
Embalse	Reservoir	Sendero	Route/Path
Era	Threshing Floor	Valle	Valley
Ermita	Chapel/Shrine	Verde	Green
Estación de Guaguas	Bus Station	Viejo/Vieja	Old
Fuente	Fountain/Spring	Volcán	Volcano

Aloes and rock stacks on the rugged coast between Benijo and El Draguillo (Walk 4)

APPENDIX C
Useful contacts

Travel and transport

Inter-island flights
Binter Canarias, tel. 902-391392, www.bintercanarias.com
Canary Fly, tel. 902-808065, www.canary-fly.es

Inter-island ferries
Lineas Fred Olsen, tel. 902-100107, www.fredolsen.es
Naviera Armas, tel. 902-456500, www.naviera-armas.com

Bus services
Tenerife – TITSA, tel. 922-531300, www.titsa.com

Canary Islands tourism
General Canary Islands tourism, www.turismodecanarias.com
Canary Islands eco-tourism, www.ecoturismocanarias.com
Tenerife tourism, www.visittenerife.com

Tourist information offices
Tenerife Sur Airport, tel. 922-392037
Tenerife Norte Airport, tel. 922-635192
Intercambiador (Bus Station) Santa Cruz, tel. 922-533353
Santa Cruz (Cabildo), tel. 922-239592
La Laguna, tel. 922-632718
Candelaria, tel. 922-032230
Garachico, tel. 922-133461
Los Cristianos, tel. 922-757137
Buenavista del Norte, tel. 922-127192
Icod de los Vinos, tel. 922-812123
La Orotava, tel. 922-323041
Puerto de la Cruz, tel. 922-388777
Puerto de la Cruz, tel. 922-386000

Island Government (Cabildo)
Cabildo de Tenerife, www.tenerife.es

El Teide summit permit

Office – Parque Nacional del Teide, Calle Emilio Calzadilla 5, Planta 4, 38002 Santa Cruz, Tenerife. Tel. 922-922371.

Online – www.reservasparquesnacionales.es and click on 'Teide'.

El Teide, the highest mountain on Spanish territory, rises majestically right in the middle of Tenerife

NOTES

NOTES

NOTES

The Great
Outdoors

DIGITAL EDITIONS
30-DAY
FREE TRIAL

- Substantial savings on the newsstand price and print subscriptions
- Instant access wherever you are, even if you are offline
- Back issues at your fingertips

Downloading **The Great Outdoors** to your digital device is easy, just follow the steps below:

1 **Download the App** from the App Store

2 **Open the App**, click on 'subscriptions' and choose an annual subscription

3 **Download** the latest issue and enjoy

The digital edition is also available on
The 30-day free trial is not available on Android or Pocketmags and is only available to new subscribers

 pocketmags.com

LISTING OF CICERONE GUIDES

For full information on all our
guides, books and eBooks,
visit our website:
www.cicerone.co.uk

Walking – Trekking – Mountaineering – Climbing – Cycling

Over 40 years, Cicerone have built up an outstanding collection of 300 guides, inspiring all sorts of amazing adventures.

Every guide comes from extensive exploration and research by our expert authors, all with a passion for their subjects. They are frequently praised, endorsed and used by clubs, instructors and outdoor organisations.

All our titles can now be bought as **e-books** and many as iPad and Kindle files and we will continue to make all our guides available for these and many other devices.

Our website shows any **new information** we've received since a book was published. Please do let us know if you find anything has changed, so that we can pass on the latest details. On our **website** you'll also find some great ideas and lots of information, including sample chapters, contents lists, reviews, articles and a photo gallery.

It's easy to keep in touch with what's going on at Cicerone, by getting our monthly **free e-newsletter**, which is full of offers, competitions, up-to-date information and topical articles. You can subscribe on our home page and also follow us on **Facebook** and **Twitter**, as well as our **blog**.

Cicerone – the very best guides for exploring the world.

CICERONE

2 Police Square Milnthorpe Cumbria LA7 7PY
Tel: 015395 62069 info@cicerone.co.uk
www.cicerone.co.uk